Lowdham Grange. Borstal!

Jeremy Lodge

Also by Jeremy Lodge

St Mary Magdalene:
Guardian of Newark and Civil War Church

The Church of St John the Baptist
(South Collingham)

The Church of All Saints
(North Collingham)

The Church of St Cecilia (Girton)

The Church of St Bartholomew (Langford)

The Church of St Leonard (Newark)

Please visit:
www.jeremylodge.co.uk

© Copyright Jeremy Lodge

ISBN: 978-0-9956634-0-4

Jeremy Lodge Publishing
www.jeremylodge.co.uk

Printed by Russell Press
Russell House, Bulwell Lane, Basford, Nottingham NG6 0BT

Unless specifically stated
Text and Images Copyright
© Jeremy Lodge. 2016
All Rights Reserved

Every effort has been made to trace the owners of material reproduced within and to acknowledge the appropriate copyrights.

Any corrections will be incorporated in future editions.

Image on front cover: Unknown

Quote on back cover: Heather Bennett, 1997.

Many thanks to Mark, Robin and Pat
for their support and patience.

And, to the many named and unnamed people who created Lowdham Grange and to those who contributed to this text.

Contents

PREFACE 4

PART 1: PENAL CONTEXT 11

    WHAT AND WHY BORSTAL? 12
    PRISON FOR YOUNG OFFENDERS 12
    THE PRISON REGIME IN THE 1800S 13
    THE CHILDREN OF CONVICTS 16
    THE BEGINNINGS OF CHANGE FOR YOUNG CONVICTS 17
    ELEMENTS OF PENAL REFORM IN THE 1800S 18
    CREATION OF THE PRISONS COMMISSION 23
    THE GLADSTONE REPORT, 1895 26
    RUGGLES-BRISE AND THE EARLY BORSTALS 28
    WINSTON CHURCHILL 33
    1911 TO 1921 35

PART 2: FINDING LOWDHAM GRANGE 40

    A MAJOR INNOVATION IN PENAL HISTORY 41
    IS THERE NO RICH MAN? 44
    A MAJOR INNOVATION 48
    FINDING LOWDHAM GRANGE 48
    MORE BARRIERS BEFORE THE BUILD 49

PART 3: THE MARCH AND THE BUILD 55

    THE GOLDEN ERA OF BORSTALS 55
    THE MARCH FROM FELTHAM TO LOWDHAM (1930) 56
    LAYING THE FOUNDATION STONE 68
    BUILDING LOWDHAM GRANGE 73
    THE BUILDING WORK CONTINUES 92
    LIFE IN A BORSTAL 96
    THE GOVERNOR AND OFFICERS 96
    HE WHO DOESN'T GET SMACKED 98
    ACCORDING TO THE GOVERNOR 102
    THE OFFICER: WHAT TYPE OF A MAN? 110

PART 4: THE WAR AND POST WAR YEARS 114

THE WAR YEARS	115
THE POST WAR YEARS	120
THE 1950S	122
THE PRISONS ACT 1952	123
LOWDHAM GRANGE IN THE 1950S	124
THE DAILY ROUTINE	127
UP ON THE FARM IN THE 1940S AND 1950S	131

PART 5: IN YOUR OWN WORDS 147

THE LADS	149
WATCH OUT FOR THE STAFF!	153
AN INCONVENIENT STATION	158
THE COCKER BECK	161
SHIP SHAPE	162
AT HOME ON THE ESTATE	164
FACILITIES?	165
WORKING AT LOWDHAM GRANGE	167
FAMILY VISITS	173
MATRONS	178
CHILD'S PLAY AT LOWDHAM GRANGE	180
THE CRIMINAL JUSTICE BILL AND ACT 1982	184
TO BE REPLACED BY?	187
THE END	189
POSTSCRIPT: FORMER LOWDHAM LADS INTERNET CHATTER	191
EPILOGUE	200

APPENDIX I 203

WILLIAM BERNARD 'BARNEY' MALONE	203

APPENDIX II 207

NOT JUST LLEWELLIN	207

APPENDIX III 213

OPEN PRISONS, BRITISH STYLE	213

APPENDIX IV 215

THE ORDINARY PRISONER, 1911.	215

APPENDIX V 219

BORSTAL ROUTINE: 219
DIET AND THE BELL SCALE 219

APPENDIX VI **227**

LOWDHAM GRANGE: A PRIVATE ESTATE 227
THE LAND 227
GRANGE HOUSE 229
LOWDHAM GRANGE 1808 - 1917: STORER 232
1911 TO 1930: GIBBS 235
PLOUGHMAN WOOD 238
HUNTERS HILL FARM 242
DECOY 242
HEY CHUM GOT ANY GUM? 243

APPENDIX VII **245**

PLANNED AND ACTUAL LAYOUT OF THE INSTITUTION 245
THE TOWER 251
A LAST GASP ALTERNATIVE? 252
STAFF QUARTERS 255

Preface

In the following pages I uncover the ground breaking history of Lowdham Grange Open Borstal Institution which has a significant place in the history of penal reform.

Lowdham Grange Borstal was important nationally and internationally as the first Open Borstal in the world. Due to its long and established culture of integrating and interacting with the local community it also has an important place in the hearts and histories of its neighbouring villages. It still remains important to many individuals who lived, worked and came into contact with 'The Grange' and its people on both sides of the legal divide.

Within this book I essentially follow a timeline which sets the scene and describes relevant aspects of the penal system of the 1800's and the developing thought that eventually led to the creation of 'The Grange' (Lowdham Grange Borstal Institution, its two Farms and the Officers Housing Estate) in 1930. I also introduce some of the key figures in this aspect of penal reform, Stansfeld, Paterson and Llewellin.

John Stansfeld, through his Oxford Mission in Bermondsey gave Oxford University graduates like

Alexander (Alec) Paterson first-hand experience of the urban poor and their living conditions of which they would otherwise only have read dry second hand accounts. He also introduced them to his innovative approaches including summer camps which were copied by the Borstal system and the Boy Scout Movement.

Stansfeld and his 'Camp Officers' at a Camp for the boys of Bermondsey in 1907. Stansfeld (seated with white shirt and tie) and to his right Alec Paterson. All from Oxford University, many went on to hold influential posts in the UK and Commonwealth.

Alexander Paterson marshalled the thinking of several decades and through his unbounded energy and infectious enthusiasm finalised the concept of the Borstal System and made it a practical reality. William Wigan Llewellin then brought his own personal ideology and energy to bear which completed the innovation that was Lowdham Grange.

There were also a range of establishment Victorian and Edwardian men, who often acting in the face of public, press and wider political and administrative opposition conceived, supported and pushed through the penal changes that led to Lowdham Grange. They include Evelyn Ruggles-Brise a Civil Servant, at whose funeral in 1937, alongside the large official and family wreaths was a small bunch of flowers with the note;

> 'to the memory of a humane man, Sir Evelyn Ruggles-Brise, KCB. He saved me from the cat. Convict No. 2148.'

These and many others mentioned or omitted in the following pages are worthy of much greater and more detailed attention.

Information on Lowdham Grange in the 1930s can be found in a range of archives, books, international journals, conference reports and newspapers - such was its importance. From the 1950s this story of Lowdham Grange is interwoven with the living reminiscences of local villagers, the staff, their children and their former charges, 'The Boys' - also known as 'The Lads.' Shining through their stories are the enduring importance and pride of being linked to Lowdham Grange.

The Borstal closed in 1982: these historic buildings were mothballed in 1989 and demolished in 1996. The photograph of the clock tower *(Courtesy of the Prison Service Museum)* not long before demolition is perhaps a fitting representation of how in its latter decades, time and circumstance worked against Lowdham Grange and the Borstal approach.

I have consciously retained some of the words and phrases used during the period to provide authenticity. In the establishment and early years of the Borstal system there were strong religious, imperial, middle class and public school attitudes and phrases that are very apparent to the modern reader. I hope that you enjoy, find something new and some things that you remember in the following pages.

Jeremy Lodge
December 2016

15 Satterley Close
Witham St Hughs South
Lincoln
LN6 9QB

email: jeremylodge@yahoo.co.uk

web page: www.jeremylodge.co.uk

Jenny Ardley 2001

MSc Thesis. Internet Journal of Criminology

Open prisons are unique in their aims and objectives. They have very low security; there are no bars on the windows or locks on the doors. A prisoner could walk out at almost any time unnoticed or unchallenged by prison staff.

Progression in open prisons is usually the product of the forward thinking members of staff within them.

1955 First United Nations Congress
on the
Prevention of Crime and Treatment of Offenders

The development of open Prisons is one of the most important steps in modern penal reform. Such institutions represent a successful application of the principle of individualism of treatment with a view to social readjustment.

In Borstals we are trying to put right in less than 18 months what has gone wrong in the previous 18 years.

A Borstal Governor in 1971

"One of the best Borstals I have seen is the one built by the boys themselves at Lowdham Grange in Nottinghamshire."

Baroness Masham of Ilton.

In the House of Lords on 7th June 1982.

Part 1: Penal Context

This part will briefly explore the penal background from which the concept and finally the reality of the Borstal System and eventually 'Open Borstals' of which Lowdham Grange was the first of this type, were created.

What and Why Borstal?
Introduction

This is not intended as a history of penal reform, but it provides a useful background for understanding the progression of ideas and political action that led to the creation of the Borstal system in 1902, which took vulnerable young adults between the ages of sixteen and twenty one years.

While institutions such as the Reformatory Schools presaged the arrival of the Borstal, in the main children and young offenders during the 1800s served harsh custodial prison sentences alongside older and more hardened criminals. A regime which set out to punish, not rehabilitate, those convicted. In contrast, the borstal system was based on the idea that young offenders should be rehabilitated, then supported on their release. Another great leap was from the closed to the open Borstal Institution. This leap was Lowdham Grange which must be seen within this context as a revolutionary and high risk venture.

Prison for Young Offenders

According to Edmund du Cane, the first Chairman of the Prison Commissioners, in 1816 when London's population was under one and a half million its prisons held over two thousand inmates under the age of twenty years, half of whom were under sixteen: some were as young as nine. One thousand had been convicted of a felony (originally a crime for which the convicted person's land and goods would be confiscated) and would have in all likelihood been hanged or transported – children shared the same punishment as adults, without favour.

The Prison Regime in the 1800s

The prison regime in the late 1800s was based on the principle of punishment and solitary confinement, so that offenders could contemplate and see the error of their ways.

A prisoner's first month was spent sleeping on a plank bed and working alone in his cell. The work was tedious, unpleasant and unconstructive and included pulling apart pieces of old tarry rope and working on the crank (a wheel with a counting device which turned a box of gravel) or the treadmill. Some worked alone in their cell, others on larger treadmills with several other prisoners.

No talking was permitted. No letters or visitors were allowed for the first three months, and thereafter only once every three months. The food was monotonous and unpalatable (bread, meal and potatoes). Facilities for personal hygiene were minimal. Convicts (those sentenced to penal servitude) spent the first nine months in 'solitary'. All would receive the 'convict crop' haircut, would wear the intentionally demeaning and unsightly prison uniform and were expected to face the wall in the presence of visitors. Under the 1857 Penal Servitude Act, marks were awarded for good behaviour with a convict having served more than three years being able to earn remission of up to a quarter of his sentence.

Statutes dating back to the eighteenth century authorised hard labour for convicted felons. The nature of the labour was defined in fairly general terms. Section 19 of the Prison Act 1865 divided hard labour into two classes. Hard labour of the first class was 'the tread wheel, shot drill, crank, capstan, stone breaking or such other hard bodily labour as may be determined by the Justices with the approval of the Secretary of State.' Second-class hard labour was 'such other description of bodily labour as might be appointed by the Justices.' The Prison Act (1877) limited Hard Labour of the First Class solely to the first month of imprisonment.

Note in the following picture the age, offence and sentence of these two young boys in 1899 – almost twelve and thirteen years old - which caused them to be sentenced to 5 days hard labour.

PRESENTED BY ALEXR. PATERSON (BORSTAL
COMMISSIONER OF PRISONS) TO THE
FOUNDER OF BORSTAL,

SIR EVELYN RUGGLES-BRISE K.C.B.

as a slight tribute to his Faith and Vision in delivering the Young Offender from the methods of earlier times.

BOYS IN PORTSMOUTH PRISON, 1899 -
(*THREE YEARS BEFORE THE INTRODUCTION OF THE BORSTAL SYSTEM*)

F.P. Age $11\frac{10}{12}$ A.P. Age $13\frac{5}{12}$

THEIR OFFENCE :- Wilful damage to a door (throwing mortar at it.)
SENTENCE :- 5 days' Hard Labour, or 7s. 6d.

The picture demonstrates that at the end of the century even children could still find themselves undertaking a sentence of hard labour in prison - for a minor offence.

The following pages will examine some of the key initiatives and reforms that should have removed children from such harsh adult custodial sentences.

The Children of Convicts

There had long been concern about the children of convicted criminals and the prevention and punishment for crimes committed by young people. There was likely some narrow self-interest as well as much philanthropy at work in the solutions that were implemented: for example, in 1756 the Marine Society established a school for waifs, strays and children of convicts whose purpose was to clothe and feed them and eventually send them to sea. In 1788 the Philanthropic Society established a school in London for the Children of Convicts. The Stretton Colony in Warwickshire used an old statute which allowed the hiring of young people for agricultural work and similarly Redhill Farm School, which had been modelled on the French agricultural colony at Mettray, was established in 1839. These and other 'Industrial and Reformatory Schools' became a significant movement. There were broadly similar examples in Italy and at Elmira in New York, USA. The underlying idea was that criminality could be divided into career phases and that up to a certain age every criminal is potentially a good citizen. Thus, by targeting the early stages with long curative detention, the supply of habitual criminals would eventually be cut off.

The Beginnings of Change for Young Convicts

The Parkhurst Act (1838) considered that it would be 'of great public advantage that a prison be provided in which young offenders may be detained, and corrected, and receive such discipline as shall appear most conducive to their reformation and the repression of crime.' This Act enabled the former military hospital on the Isle of Wight to be used as such a prison for those under eighteen years who had been sentenced to deportation. It created what Edmund du Cane (Chairman of the Prisons Commission) described as 'a system distinguished from that applied to adults, by being composed more largely of reformation than the strict penal element.' The inmates could finally be pardoned and sent to a reformatory school or transported to the colonies in line with their initial sentence.

The Reformatory Schools Act (1854) allowed the courts to commit offenders under sixteen years to a maximum of five years in a reformatory and gave these voluntarily run schools legal powers to detain and control those in their charge. Local Authorities were given powers to establish Reformatory Schools in 1857. However, it was not until 1866 that the requirement of a period of imprisonment as preparation for Reformatory School was removed. Industrial Schools were placed on a formal legal basis by the 1857 Act as training schools for children under fourteen years who needed care and protection or were beyond the control of their parents and, from 1870, for truancy. Again, these were voluntary organisations. Local Authorities were given powers to establish Industrial Schools in 1872.

Elements of Penal Reform in the 1800s

The following table summarises the process of Victorian penal reform, the progression of which was convoluted, complex and slow.

Government Action	Intent/Comment
1823	
Separation for those awaiting trial from incarceration with convicted, hardened criminals	Early moves to recognise different elements of criminality which later led to separate prisons for habitual and casual criminality
1816	
Parliament set up a committee to investigate the alarming increase in juvenile crime in London	Recognition that the situation was out of control and it could not cope with the sharp increase in petty criminality by children
1832	
New Poor Law and Workhouses	Questioned why children were treated as adults. From this time penal morality/child welfare was championed by Christian reformers
1847	
Juvenile Offenders Act	Children under fourteen years to be tried before two magistrates taking them out of the gaze of public courts

	1838, 1854-57
Parkhurst Act Reformatory and Industrial School Acts	Replaced prison with specific institutions for juveniles.

	1865
Prison Act	Divided hard labour into two classes.

	1866
The requirement that young offenders spend one month in jail was removed	Increasing appreciation that the full adult prison experience did not benefit young criminals

	1876
Education Act	All children should have education

	1877
Prisons Act	Put all prisons under the control of the Home Office. Limited hard labour of the first class to the first month of sentence only. Local magistrates could appoint

Created the National Board of Commissioners responsible to the Home Secretary to administer and inspect prisons.	committees of Justices from their county to visit local prisons, hear complaints from inmates and punish prisoners whose offences were too serious to be dealt with by the Governor. The Prison Commission which later developed and introduced Borstals.
1895	
Herbert, the son of Prime Minister William Ewart GLadstone, led a Home Office Committee which slowly resulted in a fundamental change in the treatment of young offenders	Advised productive labour in Prisons Detention in juvenile reformatories up to the age of twenty three Envisioned institutions like Lowdham Grange and North Sea Camp, the first two Open Borstals, both of which were implemented by Prison Commissioner Paterson and their first Governor, W W Llewellin - over three decades later.

	1896/7/8
2 Draft Bills Prisons Act	Dealt with some of recommendations of GLadstone Report, particularly the principle that men and women should be better people when they left prison than when they had entered and that young offenders should be treated separately and not mixed with adult prisoners.
	1900
Experiment in the new ideas. Bedford	A small group of 'Lads' separated for 'specialised training' at Bedford Prison.
	1902
Borstal and Dartmoor	A separate wing of Borstal Prison set aside and filled with 'Lads' from London prisons for special training. Similar experiment at Dartmoor in 1903.
	1907
Lincoln Prison	A special wing of Lincoln Prison opened to receive boys from the North of England for 'Borstal training.'

	1908
Prevention of Crime Act	Established a separate system of prison establishments for young offenders, to be known as Borstals – an environment of hard physical work with technical and educational instruction to prepare them for their release.

	1910
Feltham Borstal	Feltham Industrial School taken over and opened as a second Borstal.

A key element in the above was the creation of the Prisons Commission 1878 and, its subsequent work as the first body to have control over all English and Welsh prisons.

Creation of the Prisons Commission

The 1877 Prison Act was primarily designed to bring all prisons under the control and financing of the Home Office. It created a National Board of Commissioners for Prisons in England and Wales in 1878. This was contentiously dissolved in 1963 when its functions were merged within various departments of the Home Office. The Commission consisted of a Chairman, an Administrative Commissioner, a

Medical Commissioner and four Assistant Commissioners, all of whom with their supporting staff were permanent civil servants in post until retirement.

In its early years the Commission was dominated by its first Chair Edmund Du Cane, the former Director of Convict Prisons. He had previously been a Military Engineer and had organised convict labour on public works in the Swan Colony in Australia and was a visiting magistrate of convict stations there. Returning to the UK, he had been an inspector of Military Prisons. He was not known for his liberal views towards felons. However, the Barrister Louis Blom-Cooper noted in 1987 that even the hard-line Edmund Du Cane who introduced the 'arrow patterned' prison uniform,

> "was not an inhumane man, but his system embodied a rigid combination of punitive deterrence and efficiency."

Du Cane was concerned about the length of sentences and wrote that

> "every year, even every month and every week to which a prisoner is sentenced beyond the necessity of the case, entails an unjustifiable addition to the great mass of human sorrow."

He argued that it was possible to cut sentence lengths and thus reduce the amount of unnecessary hardship to prisoners and their families without any loss in the efficiency of the Law.

Edmund Du Cane

Sir Edmund Du Cane remained Chairman of the Commission until the publication of the 'GLadstone Report' in 1895 which was critical of his prisons regime. He was replaced by Evelyn Ruggles-Brise who described Edmund Du Cane as;

> " ... a courteous gentleman of the old school and, on any question of departmental governance, unless one trod on his toes, of a hearty and cordial manner to all his colleagues. . . . I unfortunately did tread on his toes and I cannot remember that he ever spoke to me again."

The Gladstone Report, 1895

A future Home Secretary, Herbert Gladstone chaired a Home Office Departmental Committee in 1894 and 1895. Distilling the existing views of its members, this Committee has been criticised for its lack of rigour but is often described as marking an enlightened shift in policy from the, previously described, brutal convict system of rigid deterrence and unproductive labour to a reforming approach. It reiterated the long-held concerns that young impressionable offenders were imprisoned for relatively minor offences on the same basis and alongside older, more hardened, criminals. However, this was not just sentimental thought or care for young people. The Committee used as part of its argument an 1893 study of two thousand prisoners by the Chaplain of Holloway and Newgate prisons. This concluded that there was a fatal age of wrong-doing at eighteen years, when there are more burglars than at any other age. The Committee considered that focussing on tackling criminality at this age would reduce the number falling into habitual crime.

Amongst the Committee's recommendations were that solitary unproductive labour such as the crank, the treadmill and oakum picking should be replaced by productive industrial labour in association with other prisoners and that prisoners should be classified. It also recommended that a juvenile reformatory should be established to take offenders up to the age of twenty for a period of between one and three years, where they would not be subjected to the harsh punitive treatment that was administered to older, less tractable prisoners. Lastly the Committee found that juvenile offenders should have special arrangements for their 'after care.' The overall aim was that prisons should turn their prisoners out as better people than when they went in. The Committee also described the type of juvenile-offender establishment that they had in mind;

> 'it should be a halfway house between the prison and reformatory. It should be situated in the country with ample space for agriculture and land reclamation work *[a good description of the much later Lowdham Grange and North Sea Camp Borstals]*. It should have penal and coercive sides according to the merits of particular cases. But should be amply provided with staff capable of giving sound education, able to train inmates in various kinds of industrial work, and qualified generally to exercise the best and healthiest kind of moral influence.'

The Gladstone Report was to become the definitive statement of penal policy for virtually the next half century and although most of the recommendations fell within the Home Secretary's existing powers, and therefore did not require legislation, they were implemented slowly and piecemeal. Changes in government led to some recommendations being ignored, others were watered down and, with little urgency, it took two draft bills (1896 and 1897) until the Prisons Act (1898) dealt directly with a few of the Committee's recommendations. Flogging was not abolished until 1948.

Ruggles-Brise and the Early Borstals

As the new Chair of the Prisons Commission from 1895, Evelyn Ruggles-Brise introduced his rationale for separate treatment of young offenders which was based on psychological evidence that the characters of those up to the age of twenty-one were not fully developed. They were therefore not only eligible for reform but they and society would benefit from it.

One of his influences was Rev^d W D Morrison who in 1896 argued that maturity of character depended on physical maturity, and, that research had shown that poorer classes were not fully physically developed until the age of twenty-five: thus the application of penal laws and administration of adult justice to juveniles over the age of sixteen was both cruel and absurd. Although Ruggles-Brise believed that the age of maturity was twenty-one years he could not be convinced that offenders up to the age of twenty-five could be reformed nor that they should be spared the penal consequences of their crimes. As a result, the 1908 Prevention of Crimes Act determined that Borstal training would be limited to persons not younger than sixteen and not older than twenty-one years of age. This upper limit was raised to twenty-three years in 1936 but was again reduced to twenty-one years in 1948.

Evelyn Ruggles-Brice circa 1907

However, the Commission was slow to develop a new form of institution for young offenders. The first practical experiment took place in 1900 when a small group of 'London Lads' who had been carefully selected according to their likely ability to respond to specialized training were transferred to an entirely separate and isolated area of Bedford prison to be subjected to a different form of discipline, taught a trade and helped to lead a new life on discharge. The Governor of Bedford commended the scheme, reporting that after three months and with one exception, they had exceeded his most optimistic expectations.

In 1902 a separate wing of the convict prison at Borstal was taken over for a similar purpose. It was filled with selected 'Lads' from London prisons who had received sentences of at least six months. The fundamental principles of the new regime were strict classification, firm and exact discipline with strict disciplinary rules, hard work including physical drill, with some instruction in basic education and trades. Also included was the ability to gain promotion with marks for hard work and good behaviour, resulting in certain privileges. The first group arrived at Borstal under armed guard and in chains.

In 1903 the experiment was extended to twenty-six young convicts at Dartmoor, the offenders at which were considered to be of the worst that could be found. The Governor reported the results with 'agreeable surprise.' After two years it was decided to transfer to Borstal only cases sentenced to twelve months or more, as six months was found to be too short to make an impression upon a rebellious character. There was also an argument put forward for longer sentencing so that trades could be fully learned, thereby creating a better chance of gaining productive work on release.

By 1905 the Commissioners had decided to extend the principles of the Borstal scheme to all young offenders between the ages of sixteen and twenty-one. This combined strict segregation from adults, physical exercise and drill, weekly lectures and classes with special measures at each prison for aftercare on release. This policy was formally adopted on 1st June 1906 as a special effort to reclaim the young offender 'without prejudice or impairment of the necessary rigour of sentencing or imprisonment.' In 1907 a wing of Lincoln prison was opened to receive boys from the north of England for Borstal training. In 1910 Industrial school at Feltham, built in 1854, was taken over and reopened as a Borstal Institution.

High Court Judge Alfred Wills in 1907 observed that the Borstal prisoner is subjected to a very rigorous discipline, he is well but not over-fed, and is made to work very hard. Arthur Paterson observed in 1911 that;

> 'in prison things go at a certain pace but not a very swift one. Work is there but one need not hurry much, the pace and obedience becomes mechanical and when the warder turns his back there becomes a precious interval to 'loaf' or communicate with a fellow prisoner.'

As a result he observed that a new-comer to Borstal, who had been well acquainted with prison was 'lumpy, slack, sometimes defiant and generally out of condition.' But after spending some time in Borstal he saw that;

> 'the Lads actually work behind a warder's back, warders comments are good humoured but as definite as they are apt to be elsewhere ... if a pail of water is to be carried he must walk at a swinging pace not a shuffle, if there is wood to saw it must be sawn through sharply ... a slacker gets no sympathy from the warders or his mates. Hence in Borstal they have created an atmosphere and practice of vigorous doing – which immediately strikes a visitor ... merely to see the Lads drill (and in the gym) is a revelation'

Normal prison sentencing for young offenders continued alongside the emerging Borstal system and, was recorded in 1906 by Alexander Paterson who was to become a future champion of Borstals. On visiting a boy that he knew in Bermondsey prison he was;

> "deeply shocked by the sight of convicts with their broad arrow uniforms, closely shaven heads, and faces covered with a sort of dirty moss (they were only allowed to shave with clippers). No child could

recognise their father in such a condition, no girl or wife could believe that they loved a man who looked like that. As they saw us coming, each man ran to the nearest wall and put his face closely against it, remaining in this servile position till we had passed behind him"

In 1908 Alexander Paterson is thought to have aided in the drafting of the Children Act which resulted in young people being sent to Borstal instead of adult prisons. In the same year he became a Director of the recently (1902) formed voluntary group 'The Borstals Association' which worked on behalf of each Lad. Their work began well before release, with personal visits to encourage the prisoner to talk freely about his hopes and prospects on release. Information which had been collected on his previous life and conduct in prison was placed at the disposal of the visitor who had developed a relationship with the Lad, and who began through correspondence with friends and past or possible employers to pave the way for an immediate beginning of work on release. This work took Alexander Paterson to many penal institutions across the country.

Winston Churchill

Louis Blom-Cooper QC writing in 1987, considered that a special place in the political history of law enforcement belongs to Winston Churchill, Home Secretary in the Liberal administration in 1910-11. Churchill could have done what most had done safely before him and given the Prison Commissioners full latitude in both general policy and day-to-day administration of the system. However, possibly influenced by his time as a prisoner during the Boer War and with his typical energy he visited many prisons, questioned inmates and was very active within and outside the House of Commons in addressing penal reform. He took particular interest in youthful offenders. His activities drew as much criticism as support and in a Commons debate on 26th June 1911 he was accused by Alfred Lyttleton of "playing to the gallery" an accusation that he would face on many issues and on many occasions throughout his career.

In 1911 Churchill reduced the period of solitary confinement with which prison sentences then began. On visiting Pentonville prison he was perturbed at the number of juveniles incarcerated for trifling offences and, "with a view to drawing public attention in a sharp and effective manner" to this evil, he simply used his powers of executive release to free many of them early. He obtained a grant from the Treasury to pay for lectures and concerts in convict prisons (1909-10) and appointed a committee on the supply of books to prisoners (1910). He extended prisoners' privileges

(1910) and urged the greater use of probation. Churchill believed in the "treasure that is the heart of every man," and warned, in 1910, that:

> "There is a great danger of using smooth words for ugly things. Preventive detention is penal servitude in all its aspects."

At the end of his speech on the Prison Vote (20th July 1910) Churchill made a declaration of the principles which should underlie the treatment of offenders: he stressed the rights of the accused and even convicted criminals against the State and supported a curative approach and rehabilitation. He finished by saying that "the treatment of crime and criminals was a measure of the nation." At this time convicts were exposed to public view when being moved from one prison to another, they were often subjected to spirited public ridicule with photographs sometimes being taken and made into postcards for public sale.

1911 to 1921

In some circles Ruggles-Brise had a tarnished reputation as the Chair of the Prison Commission. He was viewed as an 'unimaginative disciplinarian' ... but was 'fundamentally a decent person (except in his hostility to women commissioners, governors and medical officers) who 'despite a firm commitment to classical concepts of punishment was at least open to the possibility that prisoners would benefit from morally uplifting contact with the outside world.' In 1911 the author Arthur Paterson wrote that contrary to popular belief, the Prison Commissioners were 'reformers of the keenest and most intrepid kind ... as shown by their record of progress of the previous seventeen years.'

By 1914 the Commissioners recognised that converting old prisons for Borstal use was inappropriate and that special plans should be made to design ad hoc Borstal institutions which offered opportunities for land cultivation and manual labour. However, the concept of open institutions in pioneer conditions (later attributed to Alexander Paterson) was not considered.

The prison population dropped significantly during the First World War. The reduction in pressures resultant from the smaller prisoner numbers led to an easing of some of the more deterrent and controlling aspects of the system that had continued from the Du Cane era. The smaller numbers also helped to sustain the gains made by those who championed a more rehabilitative and reformative approach. One view was that many of the criminals of England, like the rest of the population, were now in uniform and subjected to military discipline.

Evelyn Ruggles-Brise left the Commission in 1921. On the gateway of Borstal was an inscription to him stating that:

> "He determined to save the young and careless from a wasted life of crime. Through his vision and persistence a system of repression has been gradually replaced by one of leading and training. We shall remember him as one who believed in his fellow-men."

Under the subsequent chairmanship of Sir Maurice Waller and Harold Scott, who both harnessed the energy and imagination of the future new Commissioner for Borstals, Alexander Paterson, our story really starts to race towards the birth of Lowdham Grange Borstal.

Waller, Scott and Paterson

In 1921 the new Chairman of the Commission Sir Maurice Waller wrote of the need to link industrial training with the requirements of the outside world, to segregate offenders of different maturity and temperament into different institutions also, controversially, to 'arouse intelligence and a sense of responsibility by the gradual extension of trust and partial liberty.' In 1922 the appointment of Alexander (Alec) Paterson as Commissioner in Charge of Borstals infused a new energy and spirit into the system. Paterson immediately overshadowed his

Chairmen during a period of 'humanitarian achievement in penal policy.' It has been stated that 'a lesser man than Paterson may not have kept the 'new liberalism' alive nor inspired as many disciples.' However, 'liberal rhetoric continued to outstrip penal reality' as this was an era when, like Du Cane, many prison Governors and Officers had traditional colonial and military backgrounds and attitudes.

Alexander 'Alec' Paterson

Increasing numbers were being committed to Borstal by the Courts and as a consequence additional accommodation was required. Also there was a desire for a new kind of Institution since converting prison accommodation for Borstal purposes had proven to be unsatisfactory.

Twenty-five years after the publication of the Gladstone report there was still no sign of the 'halfway house between prison and reformatory ... situated in the country with ample space for agriculture and land reclamation ... with staff qualified generally to exercise the best and healthiest kind of moral influence.'

Borstals remained more like prisons than the type of institution envisaged above. It was not just that Borstals were located in prison buildings: a 1926 report by Paterson highlighted that the enlightened 1908 Borstal regulations were 'more honoured in their breach than in their execution.'

In the next part we shall see how under the management of Maurice Waller, Harold Scott (who became Prison Commissioner in 1932) and Alexander Paterson the vision of the GLadstone report was finally realised with the Open Borstal system pioneered at Lowdham Grange.

Part 2: Finding Lowdham Grange

(1926 – 1930)

A Major Innovation in Penal History

In his autobiography 'Your Obedient Servant' Harold Scott recalled receiving the draft report entitled 'Borstal Regulations by a Commissioner at Sea' which had been written by Paterson in 1926 during a journey home from Burma. Scott admits to having 'cut to pieces ... and ... severely mangled' Patersons report. Then:

> "A few days later a stocky, cherub faced, quick speaking enthusiast arrived in my office – bounding up the stairs three at a time – to find out who had handled his work so roughly. 'But have you ever seen a Borstal Institution, he asked me almost at once? I had to admit I had not: in those days we [civil servants] were not encouraged to leave our desks in order to see for ourselves what was happening outside our world of minutes and memoranda. 'We must remedy that' said the Commissioner with cheerful determination."

This was Alec Paterson "who had a decisive influence on my [Scott's] life." Paterson was a man who at the outbreak of World War I had led a group of Bermondsey boys into the Queens Regiment. When in France he was awarded the Military Cross and received two recommendations for the Victoria Cross. He also for a long time refused promotion in order to stay close to his boys as their Sergeant. Then when in hospital, wounded, he moved the sign saying that he was to be returned to 'Blighty' from his own to another bed.

Harold Scott says of one resultant visit to a Borstal in the late 1920s:

"Feltham *(pictured)* with its ugly red-brick buildings and long corridors punctuated by iron-barred gates, had the grubby air of a Victorian Poor Law Institution. Portland and Borstal still looked from the outside, as if they were living in their grim past, except for colourful flower beds which had been planted to bring some colour to the scene. Inside some cells had been gutted to provide classrooms and dining rooms, and the cell doors stood open as the boys moved freely about the building or worked in the shops the garden or the farm. Most significant of all were the open gates. The old prison dress was gone and the boys all dressed in jackets, shorts and stockings, a practical dress for most purposes which had been introduced in 1924 .... I could see for myself, even on so brief a visit, the effects of this life on the inmates and the burning faith in the work of the men and women in charge."

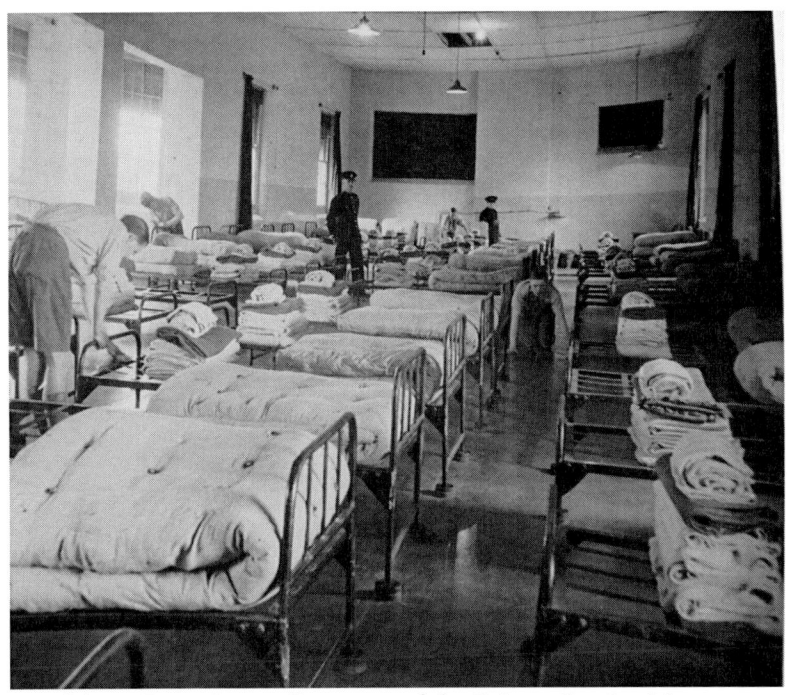

A Feltham Dormitory. Courtesy of the Prison Service Museum

Alec Paterson introduced the public school type 'House System' and attracted University and Public School men to 'change the lives of boys.' Officer's uniforms were discarded and more responsibility was given to the boys (or Lads as they were to be later called). He was undoubtedly influenced by his experience of the camps that John Stansfeld had run for his Bermondsey boys and that Baden-Powell had later replicated for his Boy Scouts, and introduced Summer Camps to Borstals. Under the Chairmanship of Maurice Waller, Paterson was able to abolish the convict crop, broad arrows and the initial period of solitary confinement. Evening visitors were allowed and adult education programmes introduced. Furthermore, he championed and drove the change from imprisonment aimed at frightening the offender into good behaviour through harsh and humiliating treatment, to approaches which promoted self-respect and training to create good citizenship. The Governor of Rochester reported in 1925 that seventy-five per cent of his boys were outside the walls in parties, working under supervision, with beneficial effects. A small contingent also attended classes at the local technical college in the evenings.

Is there no Rich Man?

The then Home Secretary, Sir William Joynson-Hicks is quoted as saying in 1925 that:

> "The time has long passed when executive governments conceived that they had done their duty to society when they arrested an offender and placed him in the dock. At that point, as they now recognise, their duties have only begun ..."

William Joynson-Hicks

In 1926 there were three Borstal Institutions; Feltham, Portland and Borstal: the Prison Commissioners warned that due to overcrowding a fourth institution would soon be required. The Conservative Home Secretary William Joynson-Hicks supported the need for an additional Borstal but warned of financial problems. In a commons debate in July 1927 he said:

> "The number sentenced to Borstal is growing, because I am gLad to see that there is a feeling on the part of the Judges and the Magistrates that they should send these Lads to Borstal Institutions, and not to prison. That is the reason why the number is growing, but I do not want the House to assume for a moment that juvenile crime is growing. It would be to the pecuniary and

economic advantage of the nation if I could be given another Borstal institution.

The Borstal Institutions themselves are overcrowded. We have three institutions, and the total average population has grown from 937 three years ago to 1,154 at the present time. The normal population of the three Borstal Institutions which I just mentioned should not exceed 240 for each one.

I should like another Borstal Institution, and I believe that it would be enormously to the benefit of this country if I could have one. It is merely a question of that troublesome finance which always dominates the House of Commons today"

Later he appealed to a private charity to provide one hundred thousand pounds to enable the institution to be built. He then made an unsuccessful public appeal for the required money. The situation is described in comments made in the Commons on 21st May 1928 by Lieut.-Commander Kenworthy:

'We have been told that we cannot have more Borstal institutions unless the money is provided by some philanthropic millionaire ...

Some time ago I asked the Home Secretary whether he was still looking for a donor of £100,000 to provide Borstal accommodation, and he admitted that the Treasury had refused to find more money for this purpose. I have in my hand a copy of the speech made by the Home Secretary on that occasion, and he said: Is there no rich man who will give me £100,000 for this purpose and immortalise his name for ever?'

The speech referred to was reported in the Manchester Guardian in January 1928 entitled 'Home Secretary on Prison Reform: New Borstal urgently needed. Chance of Fame: Invitation to some rich man to give £100,000.'

In response to questions from Mr Taylor (MP for Lincoln) in the Commons on 14th February 1929 about this appeal Joynson-Hicks replied:

> "My appeal produced more than one response, and at one time I had good grounds for hoping that it would be successful. I am glad to say that there will be no delay in starting the arrangements for providing a new institution. After consultation with the Chancellor of the Exchequer I have given directions that the preliminary steps shall be taken at once ... One individual got very near to making a gift of the sum, but I am sorry to say it was diverted to another form of charity. It will now be provided by the Chancellor of the Exchequer."

The Chancellor of the Exchequer was Mr Winston Churchill. The institution was to be Lowdham Grange, a completely new type of Borstal.

A Major Innovation

Tom Iremonger MP wrote in 1962 that that the 'always resourceful and imaginative Prison Commissioners' considered that many of the boys that went to Borstal had already been institutionalised by life in approved schools, so it was no wonder that they were unable to cope with the freedom they gained on release;

> "would it not be worth putting more strain and responsibility on borstal boys as part of their training. What, after all was their training for?"

Whilst the idea of open prisons had long predated Alec Paterson's appointment to the Prison Commission, it was he who conceived the project of using the fourth Borstal to implement the new philosophy of training, camp conditions and greater freedom for inmates with a focus on growing the self-discipline and personal-responsibility of inmates. Thus the new Borstal was to be open, without walls or fences and to be built by the boys themselves. This was described by the academic Victor Bailey (1987) as a major innovation in English penal history.

Finding Lowdham Grange

One hundred and fifty thousand pounds was included in the Prison Estimates for 1929. This was based on a rough estimation by Colonel Rogers, the Surveyor of Prisons, that a new Borstal Institution would cost one hundred and eighty thousand pounds. The calculation was based on an average cost per cubic foot, totalling one hundred and sixty-six thousand pounds, plus an estimate of the cost of purchasing suitable land. During the winter and spring of 1929 a systematic search of the East Midlands was undertaken to find a location for the new (fourth) Borstal Institution. The Surveyor stated that the sellers wanted fifteen thousand pounds for Lowdham Grange which was the only suitable property found. The Nottingham District Valuer was of the opinion that they (the vendors, Mrs Gibbs and her son Montague) would sell for less. The sale was completed on 30th April 1930 for eleven thousand three hundred pounds. Other locations considered were Donington Park and Whittingham, near Leicester.

More Barriers before the Build

In line with Prison Department policy the Borstal was to be built by the boys under the guidance of skilled instructors. However, the Treasury suddenly raised the issue of the displacement of unemployed building labourers by the 'forced labour of the boys.' There then followed a debate as to whether this was an issue for the Ministry of Labour or the Home Office. Home

Secretary, Robert Clynes, supported by Minister of Labour Margaret Bonfield, enabled the Prison Commissioner's to continue as planned.

Margaret Bonfield and Robert Clynes

Then, there arose opposition from a group of Labour MP's and the National Federation of Building Trades;

> 'no legitimate objection can, of course, be taken to the employment of detained persons on useful work, but in the particular instance in question, persons are being trained to act in the place of law-abiding citizens who are thus deprived of their means of living. There is the further fact that our industry is already over-manned, as is evidenced by the unprecedented unemployment, and the policy of training further persons can but result in aggravating an already existing difficulty.
>
> It appears that the law-abiding citizen is deprived of employment or condemned to pass his life-time in an

unskilled trade, customarily recognised as such, whilst detained persons are trained at the expense of the State and given proper employment.'

This statement indicates attitudes concerning the benefits given to offenders which were often reflected in the press throughout the life of Lowdham Grange.

Agreement was finally reached with the trades union which would supply instructors for all trade groups of inmates (including road-builders, carpenters, bricklayers and painters). There was then another delay as Treasury Officials argued that construction should be undertaken by the Government Office of Works instead of inmate labour. Initially the Treasury agreed to have only the Roads, the Officer's Village and Estate Work undertaken by the Lads. Finally, in 1929 the Borstal Association reminded the Prison Commissioners that the main occupation of borstal boys on release would be industrial rather than agricultural: consequently more workshops should be incorporated into the plans. However, in practice, as agriculture was the main employer in the Lowdham area gradually, more and more Lads worked on the land. After World War II one of the major issues faced by Lowdham Grange was the rapid increase in the mechanisation of agriculture which reversed this trend.

As revealed in Hansard in 1930 not everyone was either happy with or fully informed of the idea of

Lowdham Grange Borstal. The Marquess of Titchfield asked of the Home Secretary

> "for what purpose Lowdham Grange, near Epperstone, Notts, has been bought; whether he is aware that the buildings being erected there are spoiling the beauty of the neighbourhood and are causing dissatisfaction in the neighbourhood?"

In response, on behalf of the Government; Mr Short replied that

> "a contract has been entered into to purchase this estate for the purposes of a new Borstal Institution. No buildings have as yet been erected or started, so my Right Hon. Friend finds it difficult to understand the ground for the suggestions in the question."

One can only imagine what Marquess of Titchfield would have thought had she known about the planned lack of locks, walls or fences.

In the next part we will see how Lowdham Grange was converted from mental images and arguments in corridors of power to a physical and practical reality. I will introduce the work of another key figure in the Lowdham Grange story, William Wigan (Bill) Llewellin who, a Captain in the Dorsetshire Regiment during World War I who on retirement from the Prison Service became the High Sheriff of Dorset in 1956. 'Bill' Llewellin was variously described as:

'A big man who always walked quickly with short steps, hands clasped in front of him with a forward stoop.'

'A big chap with a pice nez on the tip of nose.'

'Solitary, basically shy, especially with women, sincere.'

'Well known in county circles as he was clearly gentry he took special leave and travel without pay ... refused further promotions ... and sought personal hardship, possibly as a balance to his wealth.'

'To staff he seemed aloof, somewhat daunting and intimidatory – but this would have distressed him ... In the early days at Lowdham he was blessed with a

Principal Officer, Acting Chief Officer H.H. Holmes ex Chief Petty Officer RN [*who provided many of the photographs in this book and who is pictured with his wife and daughter later*] who complemented W.W.L. Where Llewellin was cold Holmes was warm, extrovert and approachable ... he [*Holmes*] was equally dedicated to the staff and boys who loved him.'

'A father figure par excellence his strongest rebuke was "Christ Boy"... he used to supplement the boys' allowance from his own pocket when they left.'

'He expected staff to have the same degree of dedication that he had.'

'Deeply respected, he made allowances for delinquents but not for the staff.'

Part 3: The March and the Build

(1930 - 1945)

The Golden Era of Borstals

The March from Feltham to Lowdham (1930)

Harold Scott recalled that;

'Alec Paterson walked into my room at the Home Office one day in May 1930 and issued one of his usual abrupt and excited invitations.'

> "We're starting a new Borstal at Lowdham Grange in Nottinghamshire, and we're going to begin with a little experiment. Bill Llewellin, who's going to be the Governor, will lead a party of forty boys on a route march from Feltham to Lowdham. They'll spend six days on the road, and will sleep in halls and other places arranged by friends. Would you like to join them? .... I accepted the offer on the spot and never regretted it."

Alec Paterson personally interviewed the nine staff chosen to participate on this march. The leader was to be William Wigan (Bill) Llewellin, the former Deputy at Feltham and newly appointed Governor of Lowdham Grange. They set off with the chosen forty-three Lads on 4th May 1930. Due to a history of misrepresentation, the popular press was not informed. On 8th May, on their approach to Northampton they were joined by Harold Scott, two years before his selection as Chairman of the Prison Commission. Scott considered that Paterson 'had a good deal to do with my appointment.' He recalled that they ate sandwich lunches by the roadside and each night were hosted by the local TocH group. (TocH was an international Christian fellowship movement that grew from an allied soldiers club which was founded in Belgium during World War I. Alec Paterson was a friend of its founder.) Also:

> "There was no question of imposing discipline: the boys followed where Bill Llewellin led"

> "At intervals along the route one of the young criminals (for that, after all, was their legal status) would be granted leave to go home for the night, he was always back next morning at an early hour waiting to take his place on the march"

> "The borstal boys felt proud in the trust we placed in them, and felt themselves to be, as indeed they were, the pioneers of a great new adventure"

> "By some odd piece of luck we escaped the attention of the press, although, naturally enough, we excited some curiosity on the road"

The following is Bill Llewellin's record of the journey supplemented by notes from Harold Scott and an unnamed Lad (denoted by ^{L}) who was on the March.

For six months the 'carefully selected fellows' were trained in route marching and manners but 'I do not want to brag when I say the training in manners was not needed as I think we were a decent lot of fellows and well up in manners'[L].

3rd May - Feltham

Mr A Paterson, Prison Commissioner, interviewed staff for Lowdham Grange individually and collectively, and conveyed to them the best wishes of the Home Office and Prison Service.

4th May - Feltham

9.15 am. A photograph *[below]* of Officers and Lads was taken, with W. W. Llewellin seated, second row from the front, ninth from the left. H. H. Holmes is on the second row, seventh from the left.

Photograph courtesy of the Galleries of Justice.

A service was held in Feltham chapel 'He who would Valiant be' was sung whilst those going to Lowdham stood in the Aisle then marched out of the Church shouldering packs and proceeded through the North Gate, the approach to which was lined by the Governor, Deputy Governor of Rochester, Lads and other friends. An escort of Feltham Lads accompanied us as far as Bath Road. We were accompanied for the day by Mr Paterson, who left late that evening.

The entrance to Feltham Borstal circa 1910 (Unknown)

4th May - Harrow

5 pm. Arrived at Rochester Parish Hall, South Harrow Hosted by TocH and Reverend King. Had a sing-song, a party went to church. One Lad (Rowley) went home, another (Chadwick) strained his knee in the evening and continued the March in the accompanying Ford lorry.

5th May - Harrow

9.30 am left Harrow

St Albans

4.30 pm arrived at St Albans, 6th Abbey Troop Scout Hut (Abbey Hill House) entertained by TocH. Reverend Feinnes led a tour of the Abbey and groups of Lads were escorted to points of interest around the town. TocH opening ceremony, sing-song and sword dance by Scouts. To bed on the floor, on and under tables, in outhouse and in the lorry 'close quarters' but a good night's rest

6th May - St Albans

Washed by the river, cooked breakfast, left at 10.15 am. Late due to mishap with lorry.

Dunstable

4.15 pm. Arrived, after a march in the rain. Entertained by TocH in Wesleyan Church Institute then prayers. To bed as usual on the floor.

7th May - Dunstable

Left after a good breakfast. Capes on at Hockliffe, cold and rain. Llamas, bustards and game from Woburn Abbey Zoo caused much interest.

Newport Pagnell

4.15 pm. Arrived at the Congregational Church School Room – entertained by Sir Walter Carlile, County Scout Commissioner.

8th May - Newport Pagnell

9.15 am. Left for Northampton – beautiful countryside. 'Much courtesy was shown us by passing folk and motorists who always had a friendly nod or friendly word for us, boy scouts saluted us, taken as (I must say I was gLad) for boy scouts & even the policeman on point duty held up traffic for us to pass ... everybody seemed to have a ready smile ... I never saw a glum face on our tramp' ᴸ

Northampton

Arrived 4.15 pm. Joined by H. R. Scott. Swim in baths, I notice that Mr Capes, The Governor & Mr Scott ... were enjoying themselves in the water ... lovely tea of tea's' ᴸ at Valentines Café. Sing-song in TocH rooms, conjurer, jazz band and ventriloquist entertained us well. Sleep in luxury on paillasses.

Harold Scott wrote;

> 'the magic circle gave a conjuring display, the boys being specially delighted when the magician chose as his butt

a Lad who was inclined to throw his weight about, they roared with laughter at his baffled looks when billiard balls and other objects were produced from his nose and ears.'

9th May - Northampton

Wash at Baths, excellent breakfast. Heavy showers. Mr Childs of Rochester stopped in passing to wish us well.

Market Harborough

4.30pm. Swim in Baths excellent tea and sing-song – a warm hearted TocH group.

10th May – Market Harborough

9.30 am. Left for Leicester, joined at 11.00 am by Mr & Mrs Paterson 'who handed out bananas which he had bought especially for us' ^{L}.

Leicester

5 pm. Arrive. Entertained by TocH at Granby Halls. 'After tea we went to Aylestone Public Baths were we had a lovely [*lovely seems to be this Lad's favourite word*] hot bath and change of underclothing then a special inspection of clothing & sewed on all our missing buttons & other repairs'^{L} Sleep on pallaises.

Harold Scott: The Lads slept in Granby Hall where the Lord Mayor raised a titter when after reviewing the party he cheerfully declared "If I was a bit younger I'd like to be in your place."

11th May (Sunday) - Leicester

Split into various parties for church and to see sights of Leicester. Sing-song and prayers at end of day. Barrett visited home.

12th May - Leicester

Councillor Hicks, Lord Mayor of Leicester and Major Hempton of Leicester Prison visited and spoke. One ill officer and Lad with sore foot continued in the lorry, leaving 40 out of 43 Lads to complete the walk.

Broughton Lodge

We were accompanied by Mr Paterson, who spent the night with us and gave an encouraging and inspiring talk. Slept in the refreshment hut and catered for by the proprietors in a good and homely style. .'. we had dancing and jazzing ... lovely feed of feeds spread out on the table ... anyone stepping in would have mistaken us not for Borstal Boys but for a party of boys on a world's tour, we were happy as sand boys'[L]

13th May – Gunthorpe & Lowdham

Along the Fosse in rain and drizzle. Lunch at Gunthorpe. The sun came out as did many of the villagers and the Vicar at Lowdham. 'The journey from Broughton to Lowdham all went too quick ... it seemed like all of Lowdham had turned out to see us, indeed we had a great invitation'[L]

Marching past the war memorial on arrival in Lowdham 13 May 1930
Courtesy of Nottingham Evening Post

Lowdham Grange

Met at *[Epperstone Road]* gate by the Bishop of Southwell and others. The Officers and Lads marched in good style 'although our final road was the hill leading to the institution *[later to be known as the Old Drive]* we were not at all worried about the hill so eager we were craning our necks forward to see the house and the tents & we reached the top none the worse except for tired feet.'[L] The preparations made by the advance party were excellent - all tents pitched, group flags flying from them. Hot water ready in the bath house. Wash, foot inspection and a good meal. Dr Brookes our Medical Orderly complimented us on the excellent condition of our feet. Mr Paterson and others left at 4.00 pm – settled down to a good sound sleep.

Early days in tents with Grange House in the background (Llewellin 1933)

Bill Llewellin wrote ' So ended a wonderful 10 days (162 miles); it has been a happy and inspiring experience for all; have shared a common life, entirely out of common for Borstal Officers and Lads ... a petty round of irritating concerns and the jarring contacts of one with another inevitable in a small and close-penned community. The staff pulled together in an admirable way; a better spirit could not have been wished for. The Lads, in conduct, in good manners, in willingness, in unselfishness at all times were ideal; unpleasant incidents, even of a petty nature, were almost entirely absent. Personally the march has been one of my happiest experiences, I felt no misgivings or anxiety concerning the absolute loyalty of staff and Lads ... it will be a memory of unmixed happiness.'

Officers on the march to Lowdham Grange were:

    W. W. Llewellin (Governor)

    C. T. Cape (Housemaster)

    H. J. Taylor (Assistant Housemaster)

    H. H. Holmes (Senior Officer)

    S. G. Smithson (Officer)

    A. T. Perry (Officer)

    C. Burns (Officer)

    J. H. Marsden (Officer)

    E. Young (Driver)

    T. W. H Quick   (Hospital Officer)

Tom Iremonger MP in 1962 described this as an epic journey that was still talked about by Prison Officers some 30 years later. The academic Victor Bailey in 1987 wrote that "the march to Lowdham and the Lowdham spirit rapidly entered the folklore of the Prison Service." He also notes that the preparation for the march and the enterprise was as important as the march itself, as it involved a change in the relationship between staff and boys from the (however well intentioned) arid strict discipline and punitive regime of existing Borstal training. It involved risks for staff that had to

> "look again at the boys with a scrutiny, a hope and an anxiety which could not have been called forth while the staff themselves were not, in a sense, in jeopardy and dependent on the boys' loyalty to them."

Furthermore, staff on the march would be the first to take the blame for any untoward incidents or inappropriate actions of the boys. He also considered that "at once the boys and their gaolers became, in however elementary and superficial way, on the same side." Thus the March and the concept of the future Lowdham Grange Borstal included a high level of risk for all concerned and relied heavily on the trust placed upon the carefully selected boys. Louis Blom-Cooper QC (1987) noted that no one absconded and that at this time '... people responded to being trusted.'

Thus started the Lowdham Grange experiment, which represented a stark contrast to the existing Borstal and adult penal system.

One important early task was to quickly reassure local public opinion: consequently Bill Llewellin and his staff [successfully] made a great effort to talk to local clubs and groups. They also hosted visits from local people and meetings of the South Notts Hunt, which was and remains based in neighbouring Epperstone. In its early years, Lowdham Grange also hosted many UK and foreign criminologists, politicians and other interested professionals, including Baden-Powell, the founder of the Boy Scout movement.

Huts and Tent in front of Grange House (Llewellin, 1933)

Laying the Foundation Stone

The laying of the foundation stone of Lowdham Grange Borstal was an important event which was reported in the Nottingham Journal of 28th July 1930. The principal guest was the Home Secretary Robert Clynes. Other important guests included Colonel Sir Vivian Henderson, formerly the Under-Secretary of

State at the Home Office; Mr A Maxwell, Chair of the Prison Commission; Commissioner Alexander Paterson; Colonel H.S. Rogers, Surveyor to the Commission and Architect of the new buildings; the Lord Mayor and Lady Mayoress of Nottingham; Sir Lancelot Rolleston; the Sherriff of Nottingham and other dignitaries. However, their procession of cars was stopped by the Police near Gedling who refused to let them continue until all of the Drivers' Licences had been checked. Three Hundred guests assembled in a marquis on the Green for tea and speeches. Chauffeurs were hosted in a separate tent.

Paterson and Clynes inspecting Colonel Roger's drawings

The Home Secretary declared the 'inestimable worth of Borstals ... Borstal work to be one of the most fruitful and finest of our present day state services'; also that ' the essence of Borstal work is a profound belief in the ultimate goodness of the English boy.' Colonel Sir Lancelot Rolleston, Chairman of Nottinghamshire County Council, regarded the Borstal as a 'godsend'.

Colonel Sir Lancelot Rolleston Chairman of
Nottinghamshire County Council 1928 - 1932.
This painting hangs in County Hall

Courtesy of Nottinghamshire County Council

The Lord Mayor of Nottingham (Mr W Wesson) said that

'there was not a single citizen in Nottingham who would not desire him to express appreciation of the new methods which the Government were adopting in juvenile crime. They were all in favour of this new spirit, even if the cost was greater than the old.'

However, the Home Secretary said that a convict cost the nation between £2,000 and £3,000 and a borstal youth between £60 and £70. He considered this

".... a far finer investment to wisely spend this in preventing a boy from becoming a convict than to leave him to drift into offence and wrong at the ruinous expense of the state."

Alexander Paterson and Sir Lancelot Rolleston.
Courtesy of Prison Service Museum

Various foundation stones were laid by the Home Secretary, Chairman of the County Council, Mayor of

Nottingham and Sir Evelyn Ruggles-Brice. Some of the boys put on a 'much appreciated' gymnastics display.

Mr Clynes. Courtesy of Prison Service Museum

A sports day attended by twenty three parents was held on 4th August - the 'sports field gay with bunting lent by Mr Tinsley of Boots.' But all did not go smoothly as on 11th August 1930, two boys absconded. Mr Cape in a Morris, Mr Marsden in a Ford and Mr Smithson on a motorbike searched without result, whilst a fire in a big haystack under the dutch barn was successfully fought by a party of other Lads. The two Lads were apprehended near Southwell and collected by Governor Llewellin in his car.

Building Lowdham Grange

The Prison Commission Surveyor, Lt Col Henry Schofield-Rogers, initially planned the institution as a circle of buildings so that if the 'open' experiment failed they could be easily joined to create a secure, closed institution.

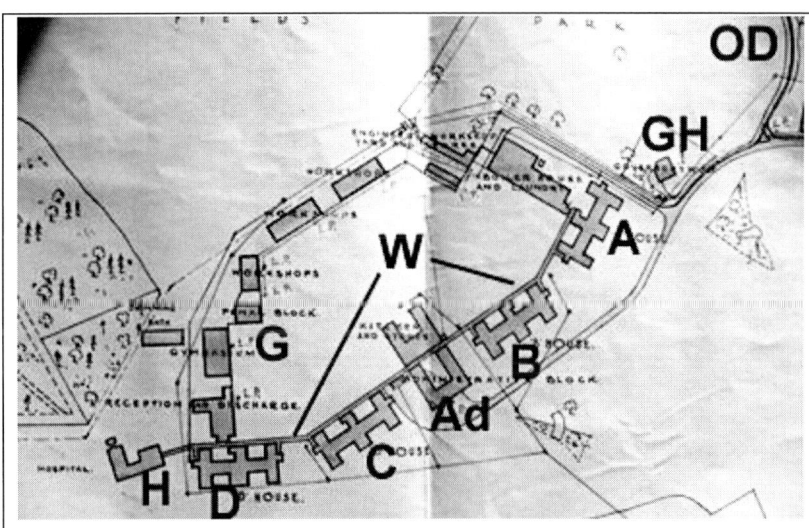

Key to planned layout:

A, B, C, D	-	*The four Houses*
Ad	-	*Administration Building and Tower*
W	-	*Covered Walkway*
H	-	*Hospital*
G	-	*Gymnasium*
OD	-	*'Old Drive'*
GH	-	*Governor's House (not built)*

At an early stage this cautious approach was abandoned. The curvi-linear arrangement of the main buildings along the brow of the hill overlooking the valley towards Hunters Hill Farm and Lowdham village remained as planned but most of the ancillary buildings were clustered in one area leaving an open vista to the playing fields and woods at the rear.

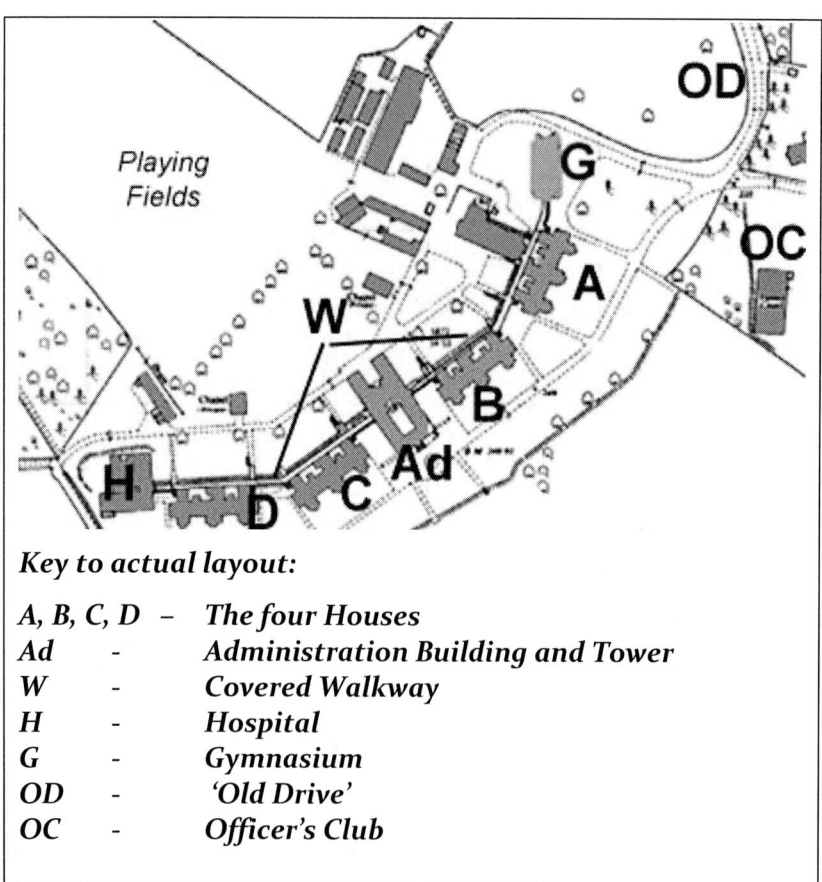

Key to actual layout:

A, B, C, D   -   *The four Houses*
Ad   -   *Administration Building and Tower*
W   -   *Covered Walkway*
H   -   *Hospital*
G   -   *Gymnasium*
OD   -   *'Old Drive'*
OC   -   *Officer's Club*

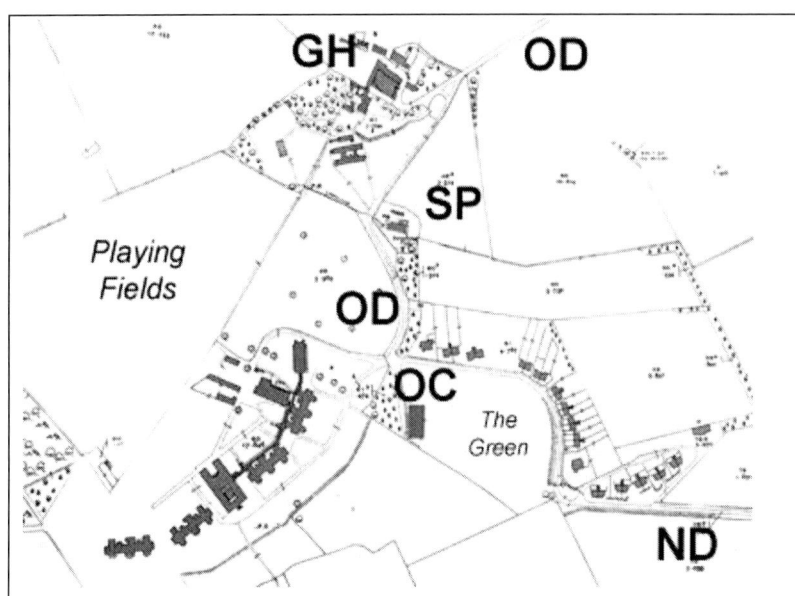

Lowdham Grange 1939. Basic map courtesy of Ordnance Survey.

GH - Grange House eventually became the Governor's House
OD - Old Drive
ND - New Drive
SP - Outdoor Swimming Pool

You will recall the 1929 disagreement over who should build the borstal: the Lads, as planned by the Prison Commissioners; Local Tradesman as demanded by some Labour MPs and the National Confederation of Building Trades or the Government Office of Works as required by the Treasury. The final compromise was that Lowdham Grange was to be built by the Lads under the training and supervision of local tradesmen.

George Stafford's family recall that he was the first workman employed to build the Borstal and that each Free Workman had two Lads assigned to be trained and to work alongside him.

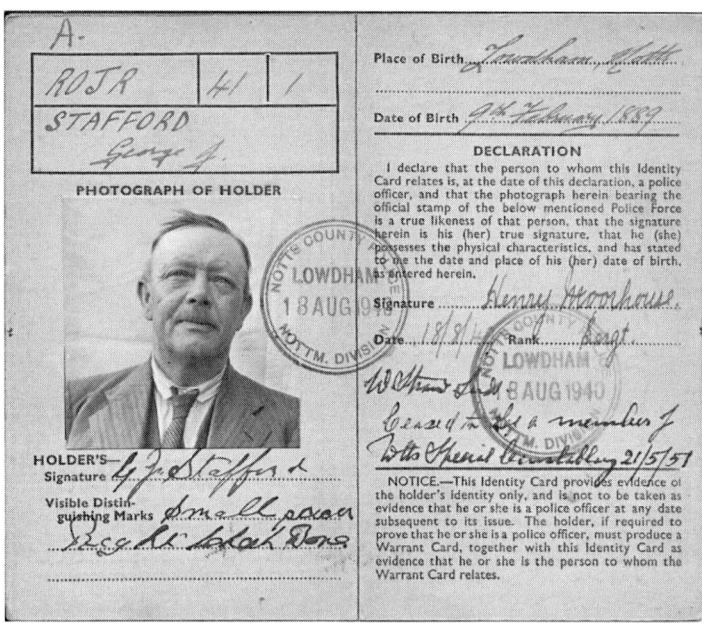

George Stafford's ID Card. 1940, this was a reissue after the World War II. Courtesy of his family.

Fellow Free Workmen included **Sid Williams** and **Bill Starbuck** (Bricklayers), **Bill Cross** (Painter and Decorator) and **Arthur Cox** (Plumber). **Bill Slack** (Lorry Driver) also farmers **Harry Wainwright**,

Maurice Jamson and **Harry Willis**. **Mr Sneeth** built the boiler house chimney. **John Knowles** remembers that a relative, **George Keller** from Carlton, was a Free Worker who built many of the houses on the estate. **Albert Smith** who died in 2001, was another 'Free Workman' who helped to build the Borstal. Albert and his two Lads worked on finishing Paterson and Warner houses together with the Hospital. By 1947 the Officer's Houses on the Green, Long Meadow and Hill Syke had been built and Free Workman Albert Smith, with his Lads helped build the rest.

Edmund John Bird was another Free Workman: he was born in Sibsey, Lincolnshire in 1908. He told his daughter that after World War I, "the flu pandemic killed at least one member of each family in the village". His father was a Railway Signalman. Edmund did his seven-year apprenticeship as a builder, at the end of which, due to the economic depression, he could get no work. Edmund's father sent his sisters to London to find work in service, and Edmund was sent to Nottingham where he lived in a single room at the Vicarage in Carlton. His wife later joined him, although she apparently cried for days when returning to Carlton after visiting Sibsey. Edmund found work as a builder supervising the Lads at Lowdham Grange from its beginning to the outbreak of World War II. Just like a civilian some thirty years later, he cycled from Carlton to Lowdham Grange and back every day: when he could not cycle due to snow he walked.

Building the steel frame for the tower, 1930. Photograph H. H. Holmes. Courtesy of his granddaughter.

The building work was hard. The photographs taken by Edmund Bird and Herbert Holmes show the steel frames, the wooden scaffolding poles bound together with rope and the rails with the trucks that were pushed by the Lads or pulled by a horse.

*Steel framework for the first House. September 1930.
Photograph H. H. Holmes. Courtesy of his granddaughter.*

*Administration Block Jan 1931.
Photograph H. H. Holmes. Courtesy of his granddaughter.*

Administration Block and Tower.
Photograph Edmund Bird. Courtesy of his daughter

Edmund Bird enjoyed his time working at Lowdham Grange and thought that many of the Lads had more sense than he had – as one had robbed the Co-op and stashed the money ready for his release. There was a lot of fun, teasing and tormenting and in cold weather the Lads would break their tools so that they could not work and would be sent inside. Edmund got frost bite on his ears. A few of the Lads ran away. After Edmund got his own house in Carlton some Lads used to visit and may have stayed overnight.

Edmund Bird building the Clock Tower, with the woods and the location of the future playing-fields in the background. Note the wooden scaffolding poles tied with rope. Courtesy of his daughter.

Photograph Edmund Bird. Courtesy of his daughter

The growth of Lowdham Grange towards full capacity was to be swift. The Surveyors' report of his visit on 14th/15th January 1931 initially recorded progress, within which he stressed that 'the necessity for relieving the congestion at other Borstal Institutions must be the ruling factor in arranging the programme of work at Lowdham during the next few years.' Precedence would be given to the 'good deal of (inmate) labour in preparing the foundations for the steel frames in the spring and summer months' for the first two houses which should be ready for occupation in October 1931. The building of the Boiler and Laundry Block would be undertaken and they would initially be used as temporary accommodation before the boilers and other machinery were installed. Work would also commence on five pairs of Officer's Houses.

Lt-Col Henry Schofield Rogers. The Prison Commissioners' Surveyor for Lowdham Grange. This was his last job before retirement. Courtesy of Institute of Structural Engineers

Lt-Colonel Rogers' also noted that much work had been undertaken on the water supply and drainage at Grange Farm, at a considerable cost over-run. There had also been excess expenditure on maintaining the approach road from the Epperstone Gate which was narrow, steep and only suitable for light vehicles but was required to carry heavy lorries transporting steel, bricks and road metal. Thus the completion of the road to the main entrance on Lambley Lane at the south-east corner of the Estate became a priority. The construction of the Administrative Block was 'pushed forward as rapidly as possible' for completion by September 1931 when it would accommodate 120 boys grouped in two Houses until all four Houses were built.

Lt-Colonel Rogers' January 1931 report continued:

- The Grange *[House]*: Has been put into a suitable condition and provides; dining accommodation for the Lads, offices for the Governor and Staff, stores for the Steward also living, stores and working accommodation for the Matron and sick accommodation for a few inmates. Problems with defective drainage have been solved.
- Tented Camp: Officers and Lads sleep in a tented camp with temporary sanitary and washing accommodation in the Grange outbuildings
- Hutted Camp: Huts to sleep seventy two Lads and ten Officers and for evening association, had been put up under in October. The Governor still sleeps under canvas.

- An electric supply has been connected to The Grange and Hutted Camp and a water supply scheme prepared.
- Farm yards are metalled with drainage facilities. The cost of labour and materials on this and the road leading from Epperstone gate up the steep hill, has exceeded estimates as this lightly built, narrow and steep road has had to carry heavy traffic delivering steel, bricks and road metal.

Huts and Tent in front of Grange House (Llewellin, 1933)

- Roads: From The Grange to the front of the Institution and along the north of the Officer's cricket ground *[later called 'The Green']* have been completed. Formation work on the road down the slope to the new main entrance, at the south west corner of the estate is underway. A four acre strip of land had been purchased from the owner of Grove Farm (field numbers 78, 84b, 85 – *see plan below*) to form a link (through corner of field no. 90) to Lambley Lane. The current bridge on the lane being too narrow and the land belongs to Hunters Hill Farm (which had not yet been purchased by the Home Office). This will enable the formation of a stronger bridge and entrance with a wider road on land owned by the Commissioners, and will be cheaper, forming as soon as practical the new road which has been postponed due to the severe winter weather.

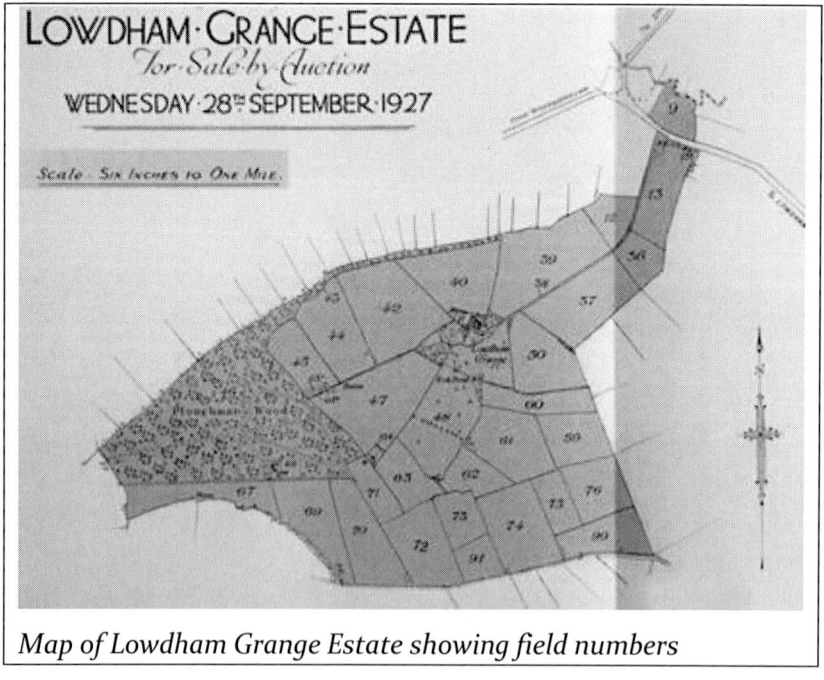

Map of Lowdham Grange Estate showing field numbers

Building the road to the Officer's Quarters. October 1930. Photograph H. H. Holmes. Courtesy of his granddaughter.

- By October 1931 permanent accommodation should be completed for one hundred and twenty Lads. Work on the Administration block is being pushed forward. Work on the foundations commenced in May 1930. The foundation stone was laid on 26th July and Messrs Sand and Company completed the steel skeleton in December. The roofing contractor assisted by the Lads should complete by April 1931. It will be able to house hundred and twenty Lads (equivalent to two Houses) by end of September 1931. Foundations for Boiler House and Laundry have been prepared by Lads, the steel framework for which should be completed in February.

A Free Workman and his two Lads.
Photograph H. H. Holmes. Courtesy of his granddaughter.

- Work commenced in January 1931 on three pairs of officers houses facing the cricket ground. Ten quarters should be ready for occupation during the winter of 1931/2.

View of developing Officers estate alongside 'the Green' probably from the tower above the administration block (Llewellin 1933)

Photographs by Edmund Bird. Courtesy of his daughter

The Surveyors programme of work for 1931 included completion of the above, plus:

- Significant water supply and drainage work.
- Steel skeletons of the first two houses were erected by outside contractors – this means a good deal of labour preparing the foundations in the summer months. A covered way linking them with the Administration Block will be included. Inmate labour will be an issue – thus the tent camp is reinstated to hold one hundred to one hundred and twenty Lads in addition to the seventy accommodated in huts. More Lads could be accommodated in tents if the huts are used as dining and recreation accommodation, and for storage or other purposes to relieve pressure on The Grange.
- Work on the Engineering Workshops and Yards to commence.

*Tented Camp with Grange House in Background. October 1930.
Photograph H. H. Holmes. Courtesy of his granddaughter.*

*Parade on the drive of Grange House. Grange Farm buildings are in the background.
Photograph Edmund Bird. Courtesy of his daughter.*

The Building Work Continues

The Administration Building with its Tower that was to dominate the local landscape for the next fifty years was the first major building to be completed. It was initially used to accommodate one hundred and twenty Lads. The Hospital was temporarily located on the second floor. The opening was attended by an 'exceptionally large' range of dignitaries led by the Under-Secretary of State for the Home Office, Douglas Hacking. He pointed out that the boys undertook a fifteen-hour planned routine per day and that 'many would rather have their punishment in prison than go to a Borstal Institution for three years.'

The new building taking shape. Llewellin 1933

The Administration Block was to be flanked on either side by two 'Houses' for the Lads which were designed to accommodate sixty in five first floor dormitories; there were to be a number of private rooms for boys who were in poor mental or physical condition. On the same floor was to be a games room. The ground floor was to provide a library, reading room, dining room, staff rooms and bathrooms. By the time the first house was opened the second house was half completed.

The Nottingham Guardian on 26th June 1934 reported the opening of the first House, describing it as a 'magnificent building.' Although the foundation stone had been laid three years earlier the one hundred and sixty boys had also built a number of houses for staff, an administration block, a swimming pool, roads and had been labouring on the farms.

The first House to be built with the ever present Tower in the background. Nottingham Guardian 1934.

Future Houses were to be opened in March 1937, July 1940 and in 1945. They were to be called Stansfeld, Warner, Malone and Paterson. Paterson House was originally called Maxwell after the Chair of the Prison Commission but renamed after the death of Alec Paterson on 10th October 1947. A separate induction/reception unit of five cells was built, prior to which the two week induction programmes were held in a segregated area in the hospital end dormitory of Paterson House.

The second house being built - administration block on the right (Llewellin 1933)

Photograph Edmund Bird. Courtesy of his daughter

Life in a Borstal

The previous section described Lowdham Grange as a growing set of buildings. This was achieved through the not inconsiderable efforts of many, including the physical and technical labour of the Borstal Lads and the local craftsmen who trained and supervised them. We must now consider what life was like for the Borstal Lads and the Officers who were responsible for them.

Photographer unknown.

The Governor and Officers

In his paper on English prisons presented to the American Academy of Science in 1931, Alec Paterson described aspects of the administration and approach to the prison system. He wrote:

> 'A Governor is in charge of each establishment and in Borstal Institutions he is assisted by a number of House Masters; each of whom is responsible for 70 Lads. The Governor is also supported by a Medical Officer and a Chaplain (in small Institutions the services of local doctors and chaplains are used). The head of the Discipline staff is the Chief Officer, who may act as deputy to the Governor. Then there is the Principal Officer, a grade normally reached after 20 years' service, and then ordinary officers ... reference should be made to the loyalty and comradeship that pervades every rank of the service.'

Most Governors came from outside the service and received three months' intensive training as a supernumerary Deputy in a large institution, followed by two years' probation as a full Deputy. At this time there were some one hundred and twenty vacancies for ordinary prison officers to be filled every year for which they received between five thousand and ten thousand applicants. However, this was a period of high unemployment and the Service was looking for 'outstanding men.'

> 'They then received arduous training and examinations at the end of which almost twenty per cent were rejected. The Officer is then posted to an establishment for an additional 2 months training, then if satisfactory moves on to an 8 month probationary period as a regular member of staff, during which he can be dismissed with no reason being given, or have his probationary period extended for a further 12 months.

Only on completion of the probationary period is he considered for permanent appointment. The Officer is expected to continue to study and can take his promotion exams and interview after five years, but may not be promoted for many years after passing this hurdle.

The general morale of Officers is greatly improved by the establishment of cricket and football teams at different institutions, and by the formation of an Officer's Club where they and their families can meet for various forms of recreation.'

He who doesn't get Smacked

The offences of Lads sent to Lowdham Grange before the war included burglary, larceny, shop breaking, garage breaking and less serious stealing (one pair of overalls, a watch, a jar of cream, a bicycle – but these were likely to be the latest in a pattern, not just a one off offence), robbery with violence, vagrancy, sacrilege, wounding, indecent assault, arson and rape.

The Sunday Pictorial of 3rd July 1932 under the headline 'He who doesn't get smacked' commenced an article with the following picture of Grange House and the statement:

'On Thursday the House of Commons rejected a proposal made by the House of Lords that magistrates should have the power to order birching ... this article ... tells how naughty boys are treated by an indulgent

State. 'Broad playing fields, a gymnasium, large open air swimming bath, a hospital and several workshops (where in the intervals between games, Borstalians, can learn a trade so they may earn a living when they leave)' ... the Estate is well laid out with gravel drives and flowers giving it the appearance of a 'pretty garden colony ... if you happen to visit this attractive place on one of these summer afternoons you will see some 350 youths and young men playing cricket, swimming or sparring in the gymnasium. Every few days a small procession of vehicles winds up the main drive bringing more of them, to be served with new clothes... a stranger would take this as a public school.' 'It is known as Lowdham Grange in Nottinghamshire.'

The journalist continued:

Talking about 'pap headed bureaucrats ... Can the tax payer afford this expensive molly coddling? ... middle class parents abandoning all hope of sending their boys to so desirable institution ... the poor pale faced office boy earning fifteen shillings per week and spending most of it on fares and lunch cooped up for long hours in a dingy, dusty, dark airless office while the sun pours down outside ... I hope that he will resist the temptation to raid the stamp drawer *whilst* these brown skinned young gentlemen, bored of cricket but ready for a game of whist or a bathe under the supervision of their house prefect ... in this delightful place ... with full clear glass windows through which the sun will stream ... at the end of their time they are given an entire new outfit of clothes.' *The office boy's mother* 'who pays tax on the tea she is preparing for his evening meal, at least has the satisfaction of knowing she is thereby helping to bear the cost of building up the constitution of the young scallywag son of her next-door neighbour ... The only qualification for entrance being that the 'boy should be a bad lot.'

Alec Paterson could perhaps have responded with his explanation to a Belgian colleague who did not understand the Borstal approach.

'I am afraid that you will say the we have no discipline in Borstal – All the Lads talk to each other ... at dinner they make a noise like the monkey house at the Zoo ... they smile when they see the Governor ... he knows all of their names and pulls their legs ... the Officers play games with the Lads ... discipline is invisible, not easily measured, spiritual not mechanical. Will you take fifty of your Lads for a walk in the City with you, and will they all return? Can you send a dozen with an older Lad to the Cathedral one Sunday evening? Will your Officers take fifty away for a weekend camp in a field where they can run away at any moment? If a Lad's mother is dying 200 miles away, can you send him home to see her and be sure that he will of his own accord be back on Monday morning as promised? That is the measure of our discipline, and it is strange thing as the English Lad is a cussed animal, easily led, but driven with much soreness on both sides.'

As is often the case there was a gulf between the idealistic liberal rhetoric and the reality of life. Lowdham Grange was no exception. The Borstal Housemasters' 1932 conference invited the Director of the Borstal Association, Sir Wemyss Grant-Wilson who declined to attend as;

> '... most of the members of the conference have visited this office, and know what we think ... we do not wish to occupy by repetition ... You all know that we have to place a large number of Lads who are without character on a market which is terribly over-crowded, and we find a large proportion of them quite unreformed in their attitude towards honesty, lazy in the mornings, insolent and grasping in a manner, and with little desire to hold a job. When they are rebuked in the curt manner of every-day life they resent it, as they had not been used to that kind of thing at the Institution. These characteristics, of course, make us and them very unpopular with employers, and threaten the existence of the Borstal System, which must depend on employers. In going through the discharges of 1930 I find that of those discharged in the first quarter, 42 per cent have already proved unsatisfactory, of whom 40 per cent have been *re*convicted ... your conference would say that you are over-crowded and understaffed; that adequate personal touch by Officers is therefore impossible ...

some may add that in the general development of interests the fact has been partially obscured that the main business of the Institutions is to produce sturdy and honest workers.'

This appears to be corroborated by; nurse **Evelyn Tullock** who joined the staff at Lowdham Grange in the early 1930s soon after completing her training at St Thomas's in London. Her nephew Michael Dodds recently recalled her saying that; "it was a dreadful place, largely due to the prevalence of petty theft and pick pocketing."

According to the Governor

In 1933 W.W. Llewellin wrote an article for the Howard Journal which described life at Lowdham Grange which stated that:

> 'It is impossible to have an Institution that meets the needs of each boy, but with a central collection centre, they can be sent to a borstal which houses boys of a similar type, thus separating those that are already toughened, experienced and of the criminal type from those who are less experienced. It is the latter for which Lowdham Grange, its location, physical structure and regime was designed and receives.
>
> The constraints are internal, there are no walls or bars, no boy is locked in. When chosen at the Collecting Centre, they are told what they are coming to and 'they will not only create new buildings but a new spirit and

traditions which will live after them' and they must make this promise:

> "Because of the trust placed in ME, I promise, on my honour, to do my best to keep up the good name of Lowdham Grange."
>
> From the start the aim is to build upon the sense of honour and loyalty that is inherent in every British boy.'

Llewellin continued:

> 'If this trust was broken, for example by absconding, the Lad would be transferred to another Institution ... a second key principle was adopted to make conditions as close to ordinary life as possible with evening hobby and recreation classes and working conditions like those of the outside world – reporting for work at the correct times and receiving payments, often related to output. Lazy boys or those guilty of misconduct were put into 'unemployed gangs' who undertook unpleasant, unpaid but never unproductive work.

The Lads at Lowdham Grange were chosen as those most likely to respond to its specific regime. Initial sentences were usually three years, but at Lowdham Grange they experimented with an early release scheme. In 1933 the average period of training under Governor Llewellin was fourteen months: under his successor C.T Cape in 1936 this had increased to two years. Up to 1936, of three hundred and seven of the Lads who had been released from Lowdham Grange, only twenty one were reconvicted and six had had their early release licences revoked. In the 1930s the following letter (this version being from 1935) was sent to parents:

H.M. BORSTAL INSTITUTION,
LOWDHAM GRANGE,
NOTTS.

.... 193

Dear

Your son has been given the privilege of being sent to Lowdham Grange for his Borstal training. It is a privilege, because only lads who are considered trustworthy and reliable are chosen to share in the extra measure of freedom allowed at Lowdham Grange. This is a new Institution; it was begun in May 1930. Your lad will have a part in making the new buildings and in creating the spirit and traditions of the place. It is hoped that he will do his best to show himself worthy of the trust put in him, so that he will get the full benefit from his training, and grow into an honest and hard-working man; able to help you and fit to take his place in the world.

You can help him to do this by encouraging him to do his best. Your letters will be a great help to him, and you may write as often as you wish. The lad will be allowed to write to you at least once a fortnight.

Your son will work eight hours a day on five days in the week; Saturday is a half-holiday. At first his work will be labouring. After a time he may have the opportunity of working in a trade party, where he can learn the groundwork of a good trade. The trades that are taught here are as follows:—

Bricklaying, Carpentry and joinery, Plumbing, Electric fitting, Blacksmithing, Plastering, Painting and decorating, Farming, Gardening, Cooking.

If you think that any one of these trades would benefit your son, it would help us greatly if you would inform us.

Your son earns a little pocket-money; he starts with 4d. a week, which he may increase in course of time to 1s.2d. a week, if he works hard enough.

In the evening he will do 1½ hours school or hobby work; he has the choice of about 18 subjects for school and hobby classes. In the Summer he may have an allotment and may work on it in his spare time.

He may join the Football and Cricket Club and the Indoor Recreation Club. He may also join the Rover Scout Crew.

On Sunday lads are taken to the Church or Chapel in the village. In the afternoon they are taken for walks on the roads or go for rambles by themselves on the estate.

The following is their daily routine:—

6-0 Get up. 6-35 Physical training. 6-50 Breakfast.
7-30 to 12 Work. 12-0 Dinner. 1-0 to 4-30 Work.
5-0 Tea. 5-30 to 7-0 Recreation. 7-0 to 8-30 School and Hobby Classes.
8-35 Supper. 8-50 Prayers. 9-30 Bed.

A lad may be promoted every three months to a higher stage for good conduct and work. When he is promoted he wears an extra star on the badge on his jacket pocket.

There are   Houses. Your son is a member of   House and his Housemaster is Mr.   who will always be glad to write and tell you how your son is getting on.

P.T.O.

> You will be allowed to come and visit your son once a month and we shall be glad to see you, but the regulations permit you to bring only such foodstuffs as the lad can eat with you. If you come, take the train or motor coach to Nottingham. Lowdham Grange is about ten miles from Nottingham and may be reached:—
>
> (1) By Clark's 'bus, which passes the back gate; it leaves Huntingdon Street, Nottingham at 10 a.m., 12 noon, 2 p.m. and 4 p.m.
>
> (2) By Barton's bus, which runs to Epperstone (a walk of 1½ miles to the Grange); it leaves Huntingdon Street, Nottingham, at 11-15 a.m., 1-15 p.m., 3-15 p.m. and 5-15 p.m.
>
> (3) By train to Lowdham Station from Nottingham (L.M.S. Station). Lowdham Grange is a walk of 2½ miles from the station.
>
> Parcels of food etc. are not allowed to be sent except at Christmas when each lad may receive a parcel from home.
>
> At Lowdham Grange the lads sleep in dormitories and there are no bars and locks. If your son settles down here, no key will be turned on him during the remainder of his Borstal training. I hope that you will do all you can to help him to use this freedom rightly. All those responsible for his training will do all they can, so that he may do well when he gets into the world again. The great majority of the lads who come here take the chance that the training gives them and are successful in after-life. This is due not only to the training but also to the encouragement they receive from their home.
>
> With best wishes for your son's success.
>
> We remain,
>
> *Governor.*
>
> *Housemaster.*

In the late 1960s more than one visiting parent told the author's father, who was a prison officer at Lowdham Grange during the 1960s and 70s "I hope that my youngest comes here." It is clear from this that the respect for Lowdham Grange, its spirit, impact and ethos was retained well after the war.

105

Governor Llewellin continued:

'Contact with the outside world was maintained in various ways; mainly through TocH, Rover Scouts, attendance at local churches, home and away matches with local football and cricket teams and twice monthly unsupervised, 3 hour visits to Nottingham (a committee of boys was involved in choosing those who should have this privilege). In addition to various evening classes (e.g. first aid, wireless, motor engineering) held by outside tutors. A Rover Scout crew has been formed which holds and attends jamborees, camps and hikes often with external crews. A system of payment in ordinary coinage for work has been successful in ... breaking down the artificiality of this side of institutional life ... and raising the quality of work. Boys were not paid outside rates, but there was a fixed schedule of payment and boys had to pay for anything beyond the bare necessities of life e.g cigarettes, hair oil, entrance to cinema or theatre shows, small subscription to clubs and the weekend summer camp.'

'All boys started in one of five labouring work gangs, starting in the bottom gang and working his way up. Those incapable of learning will stay in the bottom gang. The top three gangs have their work measured and its value assessed at the end of each week, which results in a payment that is shared between gang members – usually between 4d and ½ *(that is half shilling or 6d – a shilling became 5p on decimalization in 1971)* per boy, per week.

Farm work with tower and buildings in the background (Llewellin 1933)

In trade parties (bricklaying, carpentering, smithing, painting, plumbing, electric light fitting, hot water fitting, cooking, baking, farming and gardening) the boy will start as a labourer and after a month's successful trial will become a novice. Then rise through the grades after about 3 - 4 months at each level and good reports on both behaviour and quality of work by his instructor, the foreman and clerk of works. The levels above novice are apprentice junior, apprentice senior and improver with an increase of 2d per week for each level with improvers getting ½. The standard of improver is difficult to gain and to keep with only three boys at that level.'

The amount of work undertaken and the quality of workmanship surprised many visitors. Alec Paterson's view was that after assessment and selection relevant Lads 'could be sent for a year's hard work in a camp under normal conditions of life and work as are exemplified by Lowdham Grange. For a certain number, a year in such a camp is better training than two years residence in a walled institution. During the first two years the labouring parties moved over seven thousand tonnes of earth.'

There was also an 'unemployed' work party that a Lad would be placed in due on the grounds of laziness or dismissal from one of the regular work parties. This party was under constant supervision at hard dull jobs and was unpaid. No boy could avoid work. Governor Llewellin described the daily routine for all Boys:

> 'After the 8 hour working day, the boy washes has tea and divides his evening between recreation and evening classes (1 hour in summer and 1½ hours in winter). Technical classes on bricklaying, carpentry farming etc. supplemented the day's work with theoretical training for such crews. There are also indoor classes such as handicrafts and ordinary subjects, with special attention being given to bringing 'backward boys' up to the 'standard required for the position he should occupy in life.' Outdoor hobbies include pigeon, rabbit and duck keeping. More than 40 boys have an allotment (and could purchase seed from the canteen) the proceeds were eaten by the Lads or sold to their friends. There was a piano in each house and an annual musical production. Also a gym display team. Every day is finished with prayers with every effort made to help each boy in the development of the spiritual side of

himself which is considered by all members of staff to be of vital importance.'

In 1933 there were three Houses of about sixty boys, divided into groups of twelve. Each group had a 'leader', chosen by the Housemaster for 'his qualities of moral courage and powers of leadership.' Each dormitory held a group of up to twelve boys. A member of staff slept in each of the dormitories. The Lads ate in their House dining room and all unmarried members of staff shared the same meals and ate at the same tables as the Lads. On the staff side each House has a House Master and a Matron who would canvass the opinions of all staff involved with each Lad on a regular basis.

The average length of stay was fifteen months, Llewellin continued;

> 'whereby we attempt to gain the end – the guiding back of those who have started upon lines leading to disaster to lasting ways of right living, to the right standards of the world at least, to the standard of Christ if possible ... the aim presupposes a high standard of living and devotion to purpose by the whole staff ... Aim High and Stickability are our slogans.'

He finished his paper by indicating that this work was 'one of the finest tasks God gives to man.'

Professor Rupert Cross in 1971 recorded that Borstals were a success in the late 1930s and that well-authenticated figures show a success rate of around sixty per cent after a three year follow-up. At Lowdham Grange 'which was, in a sense, the apple of Paterson's eye', it was as high as seventy-seven per cent - that is, only twenty-three per cent re-offended. Hayner and Ash in the 1940 American Sociological Review reported that:

> "The building of a sense of social responsibility is well illustrated by the English experiment at Lowdham Grange"

The Officer: What type of a Man?

In 1930 Alec Paterson wrote

> '... the ideal prison officer is an exceptional man capable as a leader of men and skilled in the maintenance of discipline men of personality and character can be drawn equally from many walks of life and it is necessary to widen the field of previous experience, time and trouble needs to be taken in their recruitment and training for this financially unrewarding job, more is asked of a Prison Officer than his colleague in the Police Force – he is a trainer, an educator and a former of character through his daily contact with the same person day after day ... to exert influence on a human being you must call upon people capable of exerting that influence ... and rigorously train them and pay them properly.'

Paterson also stressed subtlety and good humour.

Then in 1947, he highlighted the type of discipline and control that he expected Borstal Officers to be able to maintain ....

> 'orders given in a quiet crisp voice, which seem to carry with it the assumption that each order will be obeyed without question or delay' and which gives the onlooker the confidence that all is well. A single unarmed officer on duty in a House where before, there were a number of officers armed with staves .... an atmosphere of the buzz and talk of free conversation between Lads, when 'in the midst of this babel silence is enjoined, silence is obtained ... order is kept not through the weight of authority but by the more difficult power to obtain, control by the Officer and consent of the Lads ... a far higher standard of discipline than many men with staves ... each Lad dealt with as an individual ... *the Officer* knowing and understanding him more and more each day ... win his loyalty ... the system trusts the Officer by outlining principles rather than imposing rules'

Twenty years later the Lowdham Grange Staff manual, in setting out the expectations placed on Officers, clearly reflected the original ethos and the characteristics that Alec Paterson was looking for in 1930 and in his later public and private writings. The manual states that:

> 'The purpose of Borstal Training requires that Officers shall, while firmly maintaining order and discipline, seek to do so by influencing the trainees through their own example and leadership, and enlisting their willing co-operation ... shall bring to bear every influence ... to

develop their *(the Lad's)* character, capabilities and sense of personal responsibility.

Borstal training in open conditions calls for even greater demands from personnel ... trainees move with comparative freedom and consequently make contact with all levels of staff and their families. Here the concept of the whole being is under the microscope.

Staff in an open establishment are encouraged to look carefully at themselves and attempt to measure how he or she is able to make a balanced relationship with both trainees and colleagues. The basic philosophy accentuates the need to spend time on learning about oneself as a responsible adult ... having discovered ourselves we must develop a consistent pattern of operation for this creates a trust which can be most effective in dealing with damaged or immature personalities ... the authority of the Governor is considerable ... trainees are encouraged to become involved in their training plan ... working relationship ... less intense than psychotherapy ... more positively constructed than friendship ... acceptance of the entire being ... purposeful expression of feelings ... non-judgemental ... recognising that the trainee has the right of self-determination but guiding this by counselling ... confidentiality and trusting relationship.'

Not forgetting, of course the need to manage and control the Institution and the Lads for the safety of themselves and the wider community. It is interesting to note in the above that there was also a stated expectation of the behaviour of the Officer's families which may explain some of the attitudes that we faced as children living on the Officers' Estate many years later in the 1960's.

This section has covered the evolution and early life of Lowdham Grange during a period that became known as the 'Golden Age of Borstals': a period when borstals generally and specialist institutions such as Lowdham Grange were used properly for the purposes for which they were designed and run. However, the onset of the Second World War and the changed financial setting and social attitudes thereafter brought about dramatic change.

Part 4: The War and Post War Years

(1939 - 1960)

The War Years

On September 3rd 1939, the receipt of a coded telegram from the Home Office brought an end to Lowdham Grange as a borstal. By 1pm on the day that war was declared not one Lad remained on the premises; one hundred and fifty had been released and sent home, with seventy transferred to another Borstal.

Nationally at the start of the Second World War there was a mass discharge of two-thirds of borstal boys many of whom went straight into the Army where military discipline would take over where borstal had left off. There was an immediate loss of experienced staff to the armed forces including almost half of Lowdham Grange's housemasters among whom was **'Barney' Malone** of Lowdham Grange and North Sea Camp, after whom one of the Houses was renamed (see Appendix I). A number of borstals closed.

Mr **R. E. Owen** who went on to become governor of Sherwood Borstal, the former Bagthorpe Prison, was the Deputy Governor at Lowdham Grange in the early war years. Owen worked with Governor C.T. Cape who was Llewellin's deputy on the march in 1930 and had succeeded Llewellin when he left Lowdham Grange in 1935 to establish the second open borstal, North Sea Camp. When speaking of those released at the outbreak of war Governor Cape told the Nottingham Rotary Club in 1941 that he had

> '... been visited by some, back from Narvik, from Dunkirk, from Coventry. Others write to me from places where at sea, on land, and in the air, they give battle to our common enemy. Some will never write or visit me again. They have, in making the great sacrifice, I think, more than "made good."'

Gordon Rose in his 1954 book 'Five Hundred Borstal Boys' reported that:

> 'By 1939, Lowdham had three houses built and was running a daily average of about 160. At the outbreak of war all Borstal Boys were evacuated to make room for star prisoners. There is a rather tragic entry in the Governor's Diary in which the then Governor *[Cape]*, who as a housemaster marched in with the first party, records the departure of the last column of boys. These boys were marched to Lowdham Station for transfer to Hollesley Bay Borstal, Suffolk ... '

According to Governor Cape, within forty-eight hours of the release and transfer of the Borstal Lads Lowdham Grange had received two hundred prisoners including fifty convicts. It also took in some staff from other institutions all of whom were unfamiliar with the conditions, routine, openness and ethos of Lowdham Grange. However, in the first eighteen months Lowdham Grange received six hundred prisoners of whom only thirty had to be transferred back to secure establishments. Only six had absconded, one of whom returned voluntarily and at his own cost after visiting his family to assure himself of their safety. Overwhelming demand soon caused Lowdham Grange to revert to its original purpose.

Gordon Rose continued:
> 'Pressure of space, however, brought Lowdham back into use as a Borstal in June 1941, but now, instead of taking a selection of the best type of Lads (the only major pre-war punishment was transfer elsewhere), it reopened with the best of the dull and backward boys from Feltham. This was entirely against the normal practice of the open institution, which had always been built up slowly from the very best type of Lad. After some initial difficulty, however, and under a rather more rigorous regime, the institution settled down well.'

With the Borstal System almost dismantled in 1939 the open borstals had to take more than just the 'best risks', although according to Governor Cape these were 'selected first offenders', not recidivists. According to academic Victor Bailey (1987) Lowdham Grange 'coped well with the dull and backward boys from Feltham.' Tom Iremonger in 1962, included a description by a Governor in a pre-war Prison Commissioners report:
> "It is scarcely hyperbole to say that some groups of Feltham receptions would beggar Hogarth's

imagination. There is usually no lack of variety except in the Terman Mental Age and the tale of mental and physical abilities. In size, they range from the squeaky-voiced infant of 4ft 8 inches to the shambling 6 foot 5 inch of overgrown weediness. In any dozen receptions, one Lad as a rule is so deaf he has to stand by my chair to hear what he can of my reception talk. Another appears to be taken with an epileptic seizure when I address my first question to him and have to postpone the interview until I have time to deal patiently with a nervous stammer. The tension proves too much for the nervous control of another, who tries vainly to supress a hiccough or a giggle and has to be removed, his eyes popping with apprehension at the unsympathetic tone his condition requires. In the expression of all but one or two can be read the poor concentration, the weak will, the indifference to all but the crudest stimuli, which stamp the Feltham boy".

Governor Cape said of the inmates of Lowdham Grange

'... there are men serving sentences from six months to six years or longer ... from all over the country ... representing almost any walk, trade or profession of society ... a variety of offences which nearly exhausts the list of crimes it is possible to commit ... from the minute they arrive ... not one is placed under conditions of what we call safe custody ... no door or window is ever locked by day or night ... no surrounding wall or fence of any kind exists.'

Borstals in wartime were a shadow of their former selves, being overcrowded and understaffed. In the workshops war production took precedence over training. At Lowdham Grange 'close confinement' [keeping under lock and key] appeared. It had hardly been used before the war and its use dwindled after 1945. The Prison Commissioners observed that

> 'with no settled purpose, since enlistment in short time was inevitable, the Borstal youth of 1940-41 was restless and uncooperative' of a more difficult type thought to be due to; the impact of fathers being away, mothers busy doing war work, the disruption and uncertainty of evacuations and a general increase in unrest and violence.'

This change in attitude observed during World War I only remained until the early 1920's when the attitudes and behaviour reverted to the 'pre-war type.' However, the World War II experience signalled an attitude change that would remain permanent.

One indication of the war effect was that between 1938 and 1942 the number of convicted young offenders (aged sixteen to twenty one years) increased by two hundred per cent. The Home Office instructed that training regimes should be enlivened with the later familiar call for "a brisk tempo in every form of activity, hard and interesting work, and sharp but not repressive discipline." This was an instruction that could have been written by Margaret Thatcher's Home Secretary Willie Whitelaw in 1980. This, with the permanent loss of many experienced staff who had been brought up in the Paterson-Llewellin ethos, represented a significant break with the former continuity and traditions of borstal training.

The Post War Years

Before the War the open borstal experiment had proven to be a marked success. It was thought that, although open training had been limited to the most trustworthy, this same type of training could be extended to all delinquent youth. It was expected that, when the system had been fully re-established after the war, this former success would return. On this premise open training became no longer a privilege for the few, but the 'means' for the many in the post-war era. However, this resulted in inappropriate boys being sent to borstal. One result was a dramatic rise in the number of absconders. Sir Lionel Fox, Chairman of the Commissioners, wrote in 1947 that he needed more closed borstal places than he had at his disposal due to the large number of absconders from the open borstals that they had been forced to open, as;

> 'the boys received after the war were tougher and more undisciplined than pre-war boys ... there were also more fundamental changes in the problems and personalities of post war youth, and their reaction to a middle class moralizing system.'

Lowdham Grange continued its planned growth after the war. Some staff returned from their war duties.

George Stafford's reappointment letter as a 'Free Workman.' Courtesy of his family.

The 1950s

After the War the fourth of Lowdham Grange's houses was built and they were renamed from A, B, C & D to Stansfeld, Warner, Malone and Paterson. The roads of the Officer's village also acquired names – 'The Old Drive', 'The Green', 'Long Meadow Hill' (aka 'Frying Pan Alley'), Hill Syke, the 'New Drive.' Later additional houses were built, 22 & 23 Hill Syke in the 1960s, then Rockleys View and a spur to Long Meadow Hill in the 1970s. Also, there was the demolition of the Farm Cottages near the entrance to Hunters Hill Farm drive where it bridged the Cocker Beck adjacent to the main gate, from Lambley Lane.

Lowdham Church was initially regarded as the Parish Church and received small grants from the Prison Commissioners and in 1937 a gift from Governor Llewellin towards the renovation of the Church Organ. However, one of the Governors reportedly fell out with the Vicar of Lowdham and transferred the Borstal's Church of England allegiance to Epperstone to which the Lads marched down the Old Drive on 'Sunday Church Parade.'

In 2012, ninety-five year old **Grace Jones** remembered dances at Lowdham Grange when she was in her teens and twenties;

'Lowdham Grange gym was the biggest and best place for dancing in the area, the dances were arranged by the Church, British Legion and others ... they didn't have to advertise as word spread quickly, they were so popular ... we used to walk up from Lowdham in our ball gowns and suitable shoes, wellingtons in winter, then put on our stiletto's or dancing shoes when we arrived ... if we were very lucky we would be able get a lift home from one of the few people who had cars.'

The Prisons Act 1952

The Prisons Act of 1952 confirmed the key role of Borstals in the Criminal Justice System. Section 43 of the Act stated that the Secretary of State may provide;

(a) **Remand Centres**, that is to say places for the detention of persons not less than fourteen but under twenty-one years of age who are remanded or committed in custody for trial or sentence;

(b) **Detention Centres**, that is to say places in which persons not less than fourteen but under twenty-one years of age who are ordered to be detained in such centres under the Criminal Justice Act, 1948, may be kept for short periods under discipline suitable to persons of their age and description; and

(c) **Borstal Institutions**, that is to say places in which offenders not less than sixteen but under twenty-one years of age may be detained and given such training and instruction as will conduce to their reformation and the prevention of crime.

Lowdham Grange in the 1950s

The Nottingham Journal in 1950 and Notts Guardian in 1956 ran articles on Lowdham Grange which indicated a contemporary adherence to the original Paterson-Llewellin approach: The Journal article stated in its opening paragraphs that;

> 'generations of young delinquents have passed through Lowdham Grange. Some have run away and been rearrested, others have reverted to crime. But evidence from many sources clearly indicates that the experiment has been successful. The failures are overwhelmingly outnumbered by the known successes'... 'Lowdham Grange is a model institution but one which is not likely to be duplicated with the country in its current economic state. For it has cost a lot and the cost would have been much more had the boys not more or less built it for themselves.'

The Borstal was described as:

> 'an impressive site ... a tremendous achievement' with the central administrative block flanked by two Houses on either side, a large gymnasium with a fully equipped stage at one end that will be balanced by the Hospital

block that is yet to be built. It also has roads, laundry, swimming pool, officers club and quarters; ... it is hard to believe that this was all not only built but fitted, lighted and furnished by 'immature' boys. As Lowdham Grange takes boys who are immature Lads – young Lads of poor make-up, the homeless and generally under-privileged: those who require a homely atmosphere'.

At this stage Lowdham Grange accommodated two hundred and fifty boys and had a staff of fifty. The following undated and unattributed photographs show scenes that would certainly have increased the image of privilege. These were probably taken in the mid 1950s, for the Coronation, or soon after. The author does not recall the brick archway or the wooden fencing around a track in the early 1960s.

The House colours were: Stansfeld - Yellow, Warner – Blue, Malone – Red, Paterson – Green.

In 1956 the Governor, Mr **A J Scriven** with 25 years of service, mainly in borstals, was described by the Nottingham Guardian as a' shrewd handler of boys.'

The Daily Routine

Dennis Atkins recalled that in the 1960s & 70s the basic daily routine started with wake-up at 6.45 am; breakfast at 7.15 am then Parade in work party order at 8.00 am. Any officer who was late could expect a public dressing down from the duty Principal Officer or the Chief. After checking numbers each party was smartly marched off to work. New 'receptions' would return to their House for cleaning duties and others to the workshops for their vocational courses in bricklaying, plastering, painting and decorating or plumbing.

Those on the borstal grounds would return to their House for lunch then back out again until tea at 5.30 pm. The evenings were spent in classes and gym lessons then socialising in the House until bed at 9.00 pm. Saturday morning was House cleaning followed by inspection by the Chief or Governor and everything had to be meticulous! The best House each week received a prize of sweets and goodies but more importantly 'bragging rights'. Saturday afternoon was sports and family visits as was Sunday afternoon. Sunday morning was Church for all.

The diet details *(see Appendix V)* for Lads was the same meals that officers would share, and the associated 'Bell Scale' or timetable shows how closely the life of both officers and Lads was regulated throughout the day and week for fifty two weeks of the year. The detail in the appendix is from an undated document from the 1940s or 1950s. It is very similar to the diet of Prisoners reported by Arthur Paterson in 1911. As can be seen, bread and potatoes dominate.

The Bells

A brass bell hung in each House outside the office: when this was rung the Lads had to react immediately. There were bells rung at standard times each day such as for Lads to get up, the end of work etc. However, the bell was also rung for other purposes such as immediate roll call. The bell also regulated and notified a change in activity by the officers *(see Appendix V)*.

In the absence of much direct information from former Lowdham Grange Lads I offer the following from Cross (1971) to fill this gap in our narrative. Although it is about a day in the life of a closed borstal, much will be similar to Lowdham Grange.

Essay by a Trainee at Huntercombe Borstal – A Day in a Closed Borstal

5:30 am

I wake at the sound of the night watchman doing his rounds, unbolting doors or turning lights on, loud ringing of the bell and staff coming on duty, for the every morning process of unlocking our doors. I arise from my bed, slip into my working trousers and slippers, make up my blankets into a tidy box, sweep my floor if feeling energetic, just in time for my door being unlocked, take my towel and soap then it's off to do my morning toilets. (The kitchen staff were unlocked at 5:30 am).

7:00 am

Bell rings for breakfast. Boots over my shoulder I sleepily trudge off to breakfast. After break the very monotonous twice a day parade then it is off to work. Arrive at work at 8.00 o'clock to start another day of my four-month plastering course. Five minutes' conversation with the Lads concerning the previous day's happening or the weekend sports and film. This starts the ball rolling. A few words from our instructor and my day's work is set out for me.

10:00 am

Bell rings for a tea break. If fortunate enough to have saved some tobacco I have a smoke and read a few pages of my book. Ten minutes and it's back to work and before I know where I am it is time for lunch. I change out of my boots and overalls. Then back to the wing, this is the most important part of the day or should I say the biggest event of the day. Either it puts me in a good mood for the rest of the week or else a bad mood for the rest of the day, depending or not on whether I get any mail.

11:50 am

Bell rings for lunch.

1:00 pm

Back on parade and it is off to complete my day of something that if given a chance will help me through life.

4:15 pm

A word from the instructor and it's off with boots, on with shoes and back to the wing after cleaning my tools of course. After watering my plants and crossing another day off my calendar I have a wash and change ready for tea.

6:45 pm

Join the congregation round the blackboard at the wing centre. Then it's off for tea.

After tea it's classes until eight when it's suppertime so it's back to the wing. After supper I answer my mail. Then watch television until ten past nine which is bed time. The Officers lock us away. After making my bed and saying my prayers I will start to read my book and this is when I start feeling sorry for myself.

10:00 pm

Lights out. I slowly drift into a dream concerning my previous life or my future life.

Up on the Farm in the 1940s and 1950s

Governor Cape in a 1941 speech to Nottingham Rotary Club highlighted Lowdham Grange's 'Home Front' War effort:

> 'On our five hundred acre farm we have really let go'; the additional fifty acres of grassland brought under the plough had produced splendid cereal crops, dairy and fat stock herds of cattle have been increased and at the same time had kept their quality. And, on land that we had been advised would yield nothing 'we have produced magnificent crops – particularly carrots and, yes onions!'

In the 1950s the Nottingham Guardian said that the borstal was 'justifiably proud' of its two farms.

Foreman **Henry Sharman** was busy running the farms, teaching trainees and organising vocational training in agriculture. In the 1950s, they continued to successfully run a dairy herd of Ayrshires, an Aberdeen-Angus beef herd, pigs and half a dozen Suffolk Horses to share the work of the tractors. The farms produce feedstuff for their herds, food for prisons and rhubarb which went to Holloway Prison where the women made jam. Some Lads cycled out to work on local farms and when the journalist visited, fifty were 'outside' potato picking. There was also a Young Farmers Club led by the head cowman. Arnold Boy Scouts used to camp near to the farm.

Maurice Jamson had worked at Hunters Hill Farm, since 1926 and with **Harry Wainwright** in 1997 he received the Imperial Service Medal for fifty years of service. They were offered employment contracts with the Prison Service when the farm estates were bought. Maurice's daughter, **Margaret** recalls living at Hunters Hill Cottages next to the old bridge over the Cocker Beck to Lambley Lane in the 1940s. Maurice had previously lived at Ploughman Wood Farm. Having no electricity and an outside toilet at Hunters Hill Cottages they moved up to Hunters Hill Farm in 1948. Although equipped with better facilities their new cottage like many on the estate still had a bath in the kitchen over which a board was placed to form a table.

The road to Hunters Hill Farm from the Cocker Beck (2013). The Borstal was off the picture to the right. This was the last part of Margaret Jamson and her sister's unescorted walk home from Lowdham Church of England Primary School.

Margaret recalls that in the 1950s, her father used to sow the fields with a yoke across his shoulders holding a bucket in front from which he would broadcast the seed by hand. They would 'open up' the field margins with a scythe to enable access for the Suffolk Punch horses and later a tractor drawn reaper and binder. Awkward corners inaccessible to machinery were also scythed. The stooks were loaded onto carts which were still drawn by horses for many years after tractors were first used for reaping. On the farm, haystacks were built - with Maurice and his colleagues thatching each haystack roof.

Ben and Jim Brumfield would come up from Gonalston to thresh the corn which would be either bagged or left loose to be stored in the Granary.

Working the Fields. 1937. Photographer unknown.

The two farms had a history of success at livestock shows and at market. At the 1954 Nottingham Fat Stock Show under Bailiff Mr **C.E. Blagg** Lowdham Grange won: second prize for the best matched Pair of Heifers, first with an Aberdeen Angus Heifer and first for the best of food bred by exhibitor.

Nottingham Fat Stock Show 1954: matched pair of Heifers

Maurice Jamson with a prize Bull. 1949

Those Committed for Borstal Training

In 1971 the academic Barlow produced a profile of the likely background of a borstal Lad which gives an indication of what both the officers and the Lads themselves were working against:

> The average trainee will have suffered from a deprived home background, where the death of a parent, divorce, separation, illness or economic difficulties will be salient factors. At least 45% will be from families of 5 or more and 1 in 10 are illegitimate. They have received less education, in terms of standards reached than their peers and are likely to have been in low paid jobs. As it is, Borstals are simply staging posts in a long line of custodial institutions with two thirds already having been in approved schools. Society has already given them a rough time and Borstals are working against ever increasing odds. Things are not as they were in the happy pre-war days of Paterson, when pre-war boys with today's record would have gone to Prison not Borstal. Today Borstals are getting boys as a last resort, at a point when all extra-institutional methods have failed and then they have them for too short a time.

Lowdham Grange in the 1970s was the national centre for eneuretics (bed wetting), with about forty Lads suffering with this condition at any one time. **Dr Lake**, Lowdham Grange's psychologist worked with such Lads who were woken at set times during the night to go to the toilet. Bed wetting was not a punishable offence but hiding the fact was. If a Lad wet his bed he was expected to get up, change his bed, shower and put on fresh pyjamas – nothing said.

There was a case recalled that in the 1970s of a Lad who suffered so badly from anxiety, this resulted in him having difficulty controlling his bowels: even an officer calling him unexpectedly could cause an event. On church parade the Lad usually sat at the back of Epperstone Church so that he could make a quick exit and return to the borstal unescorted if needs be. However, a story is told that he finally sat in the body of the church with the rest and on one occasion during prayers the response to the vicar's "deliver us from evil" was "deliver us from ### he has just s**! himself" at which the church erupted – well, the Lowdham Grange contingent anyway! As fate would have it this was the moment when Governor **Chilvers** walked in. His response was not reported: suffice to say that he was not amused.

In 1980 Deputy Governor **Harry Crew**, who had been at Lowdham Grange for two years arriving straight from a posting at Brixton Prison, spoke of the stark contrast between hardened criminals of Brixton and the boys of Lowdham Grange who might come to him crying in the night with a problem; .".. many have an emotional age of less than ten ... and an abysmally low reading age ... the aim was to get them all to a reading age of twelve years." However, in practice, at Lowdham Grange only Lads with a reading age of less than ten and a half years were in full time education in the 1970s. This consisted mainly of reading and writing but also other skill classes such as cookery, table setting and waiting, with pensioners from local villages being invited to 'The Grange' to assess the Lads expertise. If the target had been for all to attain a reading age of eleven years then three-quarters would have been in full-time education!

Learning to read at Lowdham Grange post 1945.
Courtesy of the Prison Service Museum

On arrival at their allocated borstal the boys faced a stay from between nine months and three years depending almost entirely on their response to the training. Visiting Justices had to be satisfied of a boy's progress at intervals of nine and twelve months to approve his discharge. They met once per month but could enter the borstal at any time. Each month three Boards considered each boy's progress. These were his House Board, the Institution Board and the Visiting Magistrates. Boys doing exceptionally well could be placed on the discharge list after nine months. Some served the full three years but the average was eighteen months. However, Borstal training was divided into two distinct parts covering four years in all. The first part was at an institution like Lowdham Grange and the rest in civilian life under more remote supervision of the Borstal Association acting through the Probation Service. A home leave system was introduced which allowed a boy to go home for five days so that he could start to prepare for his discharge.

The absconding rate at Lowdham Grange was one in six, in 1949; three hundred and sixty boys were received and sixty ran away. According to the Governor **Hugh Kenyon**, the essence of Lowdham Grange's training was to make the boys fit to face life's problems, the temptation to abscond being one of them. However he said that our 'extraordinarily efficient' local Police caught them all.

David McFaul spoke to the Nottingham Topper in 1997;

> "Of course, life wasn't perfect here we had riots and a few escapees, because it was an open prison .... We used to drive back through Lambley Village on our way back from shopping in Nottingham and spot them. Then we'd take them back to the Grange and drop them off at the door!"

Lads would never tell you straight out that someone was about to abscond, but especially with the new Lads, 'you could usually tell by their behaviour.' **Jeff Gittins** recalls that it was not unusual to be asked by a Lad 'are you going to have a roll call check, sir? .... Don't you think that you should have a roll call check sir" this usually meant that someone was about to abscond and a surprise roll call would calm them down. It was also not unknown for Lads to race after an absconder and bring him back. The punishment for absconding was a loss of two months' remission or 'lost time.' There was no group punishment resulting from an absconding. However, if the atmosphere was starting to get out of hand there would be a general clampdown on freedoms and privileges for a week or two until things calmed down. This would also happen if for example, as in 1974, drugs were found at

Lowdham Grange. But this meant a little rollup, not the hard drugs or organised distribution that is common nowadays. And, in this case the whole Institution's privileges were taken away for a few days.

There was one occasion in the 1970s when the Officer in Charge of a House was tipped off that a Lad had 'done a runner'. So the bell was rung for roll call, at which all of the Lads had to assemble within one minute. This confirmed that one was missing. The next morning the Lads got up and breakfasted, went to the locker room, dressed for work and when roll was called and they assembled on the parade ground as usual. After several counts it was confirmed that they had a full roll. When his name was called the absconding boy stepped smartly forward. After spending a cold and scared night hiding in Ploughman Wood he had sneaked back into the locker room to join his fellow inmates. The Officer in Charge had to pretend to be angry but felt that he had probably suffered enough.

At night, for each House of around seventy Lads, there were only two officers on duty, 'sleeping in' whilst a civilian night watchman did his rounds. If a Lad did abscond then there would be a knock at the 'off duty' officers' front doors across the estate and they would be taken by van (the 'Pantechnicon') to be deposited usually alone in the villages or at key local points such as roundabouts and Gunthorpe Bridge - to wait for the unwary absconder or the van to pick them up again. In the 1960's they were given 'tuppence' (2d) so that they could use the local payphone to call to Lowdham Grange.

However, there was no need for a call-out when two Lads tried to rob Knowles Garage at the bottom of the Old Drive. **John Knowles**, son of the garage owner recalls that when he was a boy, one Sunday in the early 1950's during parade to Epperstone Church, officer **Bill Jackson** overheard two Lads saying that they could do that house some night. He warned them that John's dad had a shot gun. He also had a wooden leg and always kept the leg and shotgun by his bed. "Anyway, one night" John said

> "I heard a noise in the garden, fetched my dad who loaded his shot gun as he came to my room we opened the window, shouted then fired off both barrels over their heads. Well ... they didn't get out through the holes in the hedge that they had come in through but made two new ones and cut themselves so badly in the process that they returned to The Grange and spent a week in hospital."

It seems that Paterson's concept and recruitment policy of twenty years earlier had been maintained, as

Governor Kenyon was described as a family man with sixteen years' borstal service

> 'his brisk efficiency is not of the jerky, hustle type, but that of an experienced administrator who does not drive and intimidate but leads, persuades and influences.'

The staff did not wear uniforms and mixed freely with the boys. All officers were addressed as 'Sir' but this was not required to be combined with a jump to attention. The boys were encouraged to regard officers as friends who could be approached at any time to help them, and in return staff were expected to be willing to help.

> "The Governor and staff regard their work as a 'creative mission' ... to 'mould and develop good characters in eighteen months after the shortcomings and temptations of eighteen years of life.'"

Again, harking back to Paterson's early conclusions and experiences, the journalist wrote

> 'very few have had a normal and healthy upbringing ... the majority from crowded homes and streets of the largest cities ... with lack of parental love and control ... many brought up in other institutions ... some cannot read or write ... society has not given them a chance'

The Nottinghamshire Guardian in 1956 described Lowdham Grange as having a barrack-like touch in parts but overall had the atmosphere of a school and now had four houses and two hundred and forty inmates. A 1980 Nottingham Evening Post article described the contrats with some areas like the visiting rooms 'cheerful with photographs of the gym team's exploits' but other areas included echoing corridors, typical of pre-war buildings, gloss painted walls, stone floors and no promise of comfort in the rooms beyond; ... 'the bathroom has rows of baths with no cubicles – no privacy here or in the dormitories.'

In 1972 Governor **Bernard 'Bunny' Chilvers** (given this nickname because of the number of children he had) described the 'restrictions' as less harsh than those at his boarding school, some fifty years earlier. **Mike Armstrong** recalled the often repeated story about **Cyril Checkley** who having taken up the position of Education Officer at Lowdham after a career in the Navy, gave his wife a tour of the establishment. Her comment was to the effect, "Why ever have we been spending so much on boarding school for our own boys for so many years?"

The History of the North Nottinghamshire Hockey Club records that in the 1950s:
> South Nottingham would take us to the Flying Horse for High Tea. It was a different story at Lowdham Grange Borstal Institution, where the inmates were only too happy to tell you what they were 'in for.' The tea always looked and tasted vile and was invariably luke-warm. If

you couldn't manage the refreshments they were quickly snaffled by the inmates. There were no showers, just two long rows of baths. The snag was there was never a bath-plug to be found anywhere and you couldn't even take your own, they were twice the normal size – so we just had to bung'em up with loo paper.

Lowdham Grange participated in 'two Notts Soccer Leagues and other outdoor activities included rugger, hockey, cross-country, athletics, swimming and … canoeing on the Trent.' It also had a seventy-strong Army Cadet Force Company attached to the Sherwood Foresters. The Commanding Officer was Housemaster **Arthur Kearns**. This company was finally closed in the late 1970s following the campaigning of Mary Whitehouse, who objected to criminals' being taught 'military matters' … *I assume she meant how to kill?* Colonel Gunn, the Commandant of the Nottinghamshire Army Cadet Force who had inspected the detachment many times, recalled that it was 'well run and entirely officered by borstal staff.' He considered that 'the self-discipline and self-confidence that the Cadet Force gave to the youngsters, both good and bad – went a long way to making them good citizens.' The summer camps that were inspired by John Stansfeld were still in place in the 1970s.

The American academic Charles Heilman (1978) recorded that the First United Nations Congress on the Prevention of Crime and the Treatment of Offenders that was held in 1955, endorsed open prisons: he recommended that their use be extended 'to the largest possible number of prisoners' as they represented 'one of the most successful applications of the principle of individualisation of penalties with a view to social readjustment.' But this pronouncement came as no news to the English, for when it was made Lowdham Grange had been functioning successfully for a quarter of a century.

Part 5: In Your Own Words

This section is based upon discussions and email exchanges with a wide range of people who had spent time within Lowdham Grange or who knew it from the outside. It is amazing how clear some of the memories and feelings for this place have persisted over many decades.

Ann Welsh was a nurse at Nottingham General Hospital in 1960. She recalled in 2013 that her only contact with Lowdham Grange was when:

"We admitted a Lad from Lowdham Grange Borstal who had fallen through a glass window. He was very withdrawn and had a crippled hand. The ward was full of coal miners with hearts as big as buckets who took him under their wing and helped to bring him out of his shell. We had him for a month and he had no family or other visitors or attempts to contact him apart from two officers from Lowdham Grange who came faithfully twice every week. They were very interested and supportive of him and were the only people who seemed to care. We had a birthday party for him on the ward and he had presents from Lowdham Grange. He flourished with this attention from the miners and the borstal staff. He even agreed to have an operation on his hand. I had no other contact with Lowdham Grange but still think of him every time we drive past the gates on the road from Lowdham to Lambley."

The Lads

Some Officers' views included:

"They only go straight if they are determined to go straight."

"One Lad was twenty one and was part of a gang who raided a warehouse, being the youngest he was sent to borstal, they got away with one hundred and fifty thousand pounds, his share was forty thousand. "I got twelve months here. Where else could I get forty thousand pounds for twelve months work" (this was in the 1960's!). He was a very nice youth, very good, he got out in seven months. We always got reports from probation and he never got into trouble again."

"This was better than home for some of the Lads, they got everything free; meals, snooker, games etc. The senior Lads would go gardening for old people and others in the local villages at weekends, we would give them passes in case the police picked them up."

Mick H, who was a Lad at Lowdham Grange in the late 1970s, clearly recalled his time and the people that he had met, some forty years later:

"I would imagine there is a very slim chance they would remember me when they will have seen hundreds if not thousands of Lads come and go, but please pass on my regards "regardless." I remember them as good, genuine people who despite the circumstances treated you with a degree of warmth and respect which I think does have a positive impact on your character at some stage, if not immediately.

In my case I kept out of bother for about seven years after leaving Lowdham but slipped into 'drug use' and a few more prison sentences in between. Then I fell into rehab in '96 and have never looked back since. I've got an eighteen year old daughter a couple of older step children and grandkids and am now a manager and trainer in a drug service doing what I can to help people get their lives back on track and achieving their potential. It's ironic that I'm regularly asked to do talks or info sessions in prisons that I spent time in myself, back in the day."

"A couple of other Sheffield Lads who **Miss P** and **Mr Gittens** may remember in Stansfeld at the same time as me were less fortunate. A Lad called Mark W who'd just become a dad whilst he was at Lowdham, was thirty feet up a drainpipe whilst trying to break into a clothes shop and died when it came away from the wall. Another Lad originally from London, Paul 'Cockney' L, I heard committed suicide in the early 1980s."

"Regarding inmates informing staff of people planning absconding this would have been seen as grassing by the majority of Lads and not something many would do. Anyone known to have grassed would have definitely got a beating and would be ostracised. I suspect, as borstal was a six month to two year sentence with around ten month being the default initial release date, the potential of getting time back would be a major reason for people informing. Although a few did abscond or attempt to abscond whilst I was there I never knew about any and I think people who were planning it would wisely keep that to themselves as much as possible. I think to be fair most Lads would have tried to advise against anyone doing it and suggested it was a stupid thing to do as they would have time added to their sentence. Quite a few who did were shipped out to closed borstals although a few were allowed to come back who had previously been well behaved."

"I'd been on remand at Thorpe Arch in Wetherby since January, sentenced in March and spent a couple of weeks in Armley Jail before being sent to Strangeways for allocation. Strangeways was a particularly bad place at that time so I would have been happy to go anywhere. A friend of mine had been to Hadfield Borstal in Doncaster and spoke really highly of the place. He advised me to tell the Allocation Board that I really liked farming and they would send me there. Anyway when I was in front of the panel I waxed lyrical of my love for all things farming. I personally can't think of any occupation worse than farming but was really sold on Hadfield being a good place to be. Anyway, I was told by the panel that as I loved farming so much they would send me to a place with two farms, Lowdham Grange! So, that was that! I'd never heard of it but speaking to some of the Lads on the wing they said it was decent place and not too far away from Sheffield for visits. So it could have been worse I guessed but I wasn't relishing the thought of any farming."

"I remember getting there and being really impressed, after Strangeways the induction unit seemed like a five star hotel. The Lad working on reception who I think was called 'Capper' had asked if any of us was any good at football. I'd played all my life in the school teams and played for a local pub team at sixteen so I'd told him I was and he put me forward for Stansfeld House. It turned out that Capper was a Stansfeld Lad and he used to cherry pick the footballers and sporty types to ensure that they had the best teams."

"I think we spent one or two nights in the Induction Unit and then I was taken over to the House. I recall being anxious about this a bit like the first day at the big-school type of feeling and I wondered what I might be walking into. It was tea time so there were loads of Lads in the dining room and I remember sitting next to a Lad called Jeremy from Lichfield ... Jeremy seemed a bit posher and more educated than your common garden borstal boy. Also on my table was a Lad called A from Grantham I think and a Lad called Rob from Chesterfield."

Watch out for the Staff!

It was not only the Lads or the Chief and Governor on the prowl that kept staff on their toes.

The RAF used the clock tower for training. They would fly out of Syerston, circle the clock tower, and fly back. "One Saturday a new officer received a call from Syerston saying that an aircraft needed to do an emergency landing. Being Saturday afternoon the sports fields were filled with Lads and visiting teams who were all cleared to one side and stood waiting …. and waiting … and …   It turned out to have been a spoof call by a PEI   (Physical Exercise Instructor) which would have been rumbled if, as expected, the officer had called Syerston back to confirm."   A record of Governor's thoughts have not been found.

The staff made an indelible impression on one Lad who recalled decades later:

"**Mr Clark(e)** I think he was the main PE Teacher. Great bloke, put us all through a nightmare of an induction for a fitness test but was really inspiring and passionate about everything we did. He ran the institution football team. It was the highlight of the week to play against civilian teams especially if we were playing away."

"**Mr Strutt,** was another member of staff mainly based on Stansfeld, I remember him being quite strict but had a good sense of humour."

"Mr **Bob McKinley**, he was based in one of the other houses, ex professional footballer and Notts Forest legend. My dad had seen him play on a number of occasions and said he was a great player - apparently he was regarded as the best centre half never to have won a cap for Scotland. I was the goalkeeper for the Institution team and we were on the playing field one day and he invited me to go in goal whilst he took penalties against me. He must have took about eight and I never got close to saving any of them."

"**Mr Money:** a younger guy, really decent looking with a 'tache' originally from Sheffield. He'd have a light hearted banter with the Lads but had enough authority and respect so you wouldn't take any liberties. It was routine that staff would hand out letters at lunch in the dining hall and would call the names out of people who had received them. He would call out people's names followed by a one or two word comment such as "Holmes...... Plonker! Smith..... Lifer! Jones......Retard! and so on which would amuse the Lads and bring a bit of entertainment to proceedings."

"**Mr R**: Older guy and one of the senior screws on the House who I remember being really authoritarian. Tall and thin-faced you certainly didn't fuck around on his watch. I felt he had a personal dislike for me although he probably had a personal dislike for most of the Lads."

"**Mr Geoff Gittens**: Older guy, I remember seeming a really decent and fair bloke and let me off with a fair bit of "extra work" which I'd been given a hefty dose of as punishment for various misdemeanours close to my release date."

"Another guy who's name I can't recall at the moment but I think he'd had a stroke and used to have to hold one of his arms with the other, seemed a decent sort, could have been **Mr Walker?**"

"**Miss P(*arkinson*)**: older Lady, everyone referred to her as "Miss P." She was the 'House Matron' seemed really nice. I know she was the person who I had some sort of periodic review with but not sure she did this for every boy in the House or just to a lesser number of us. Miss P had a typical middle or upper class air about her with a look of the village women you might see on Midsommer Murders or some BBC Drama of 50s and 60s."

"**Mr C**: A civilian screw who looked after the 'skilled labourers' which is where I spent most of my time working. He was a small fattish bloke with glasses, quite funny in some respects but a bit of a bully. I remember that part of our wages were paid as a "basic." I'm not sure now if the basic was about sixty pence and the rest was paid as a penny a point up to a maximum of fifty for the total of points you were "awarded" by the screw who ran your particular workgroup. Mr C.'s policy was that he awarded each Lad forty points every week as standard but you had to buy him a number of penny chews such as refreshers, blackjacks, fruit saLad type things. If you didn't bring him any you would get a whack or two with a stick and be seriously docked on your points the week after. He used to keep his chews in a desk drawer in his office and I remember a few occasions going in on some pretence and nicking one. Once I came very close to getting caught and didn't do it again. I quite liked him in the early stages of being there but gradually got to dislike him more as time went on I particularly resented working our balls off for thirty to thirty five points after you deducted his 'sweet tax'."

"**Mr Colley(?):** appeared to be late forties early fifties at the time but I'm aware that estimating age through the eyes of a seventeen year old thirty-five years on that I could be way off the mark. He worked in the education unit, balding, glasses, longish unkempt beard, Jesus sandals, cool laid back intellectual 'Whispering Bob Harris' type. He seemed to be one of the senior guys in the education dept. I remember we had to see him as part of our induction on the education unit for an assessment, I clearly remember him assessing our reading age by having to read a long list of words beginning with really short words like dog or cat and getting increasingly more difficult. I also remember him saying I had a reading age of sixteen. As a seventeen year old I thought this was bad but it turned out it was much better than most of the induction group I was with so I felt a bit better about it then."

"There was also an older guy who was the House Master or some title along those lines. He looked a bit like the Edward G Robinson the Ant Hill Mob guy off the Wacky Races cartoon if you're familiar with it. He was a short stocky bloke with a dark suit with turn ups on the trousers and shiny black Oxford shoes. He was the main man on the House and if you were 'nicked' for any offence you saw him for your punishment. I remember him being a decent bloke, he always acknowledged you and often gave me a cigarette. Despite that if you was on report he was quite harsh with the sentence as I found out on a few occasions. He was the type though that you accepted it from. I'd be interested to know his name."

An Inconvenient Station

Early in the staff induction document is the statement that 'this establishment is designed as an inconvenient station' which is something that the author is sure that we all felt before the prevalence of the car. We also felt this as teenagers certainly when we had to face the steep Old Drive in all weathers on our two mile or so walk to catch the school bus to either Carlton or Southwell. The same trek our parents faced carrying the weekly shop before cars became common in the 1970s. Not to forget that the Lads visitors had the same challenge on top of their train and bus journeys from distant towns such as Sheffield or Manchester.

Our 1960s and 1970s link to the outside world was the 215. The same bus, different route is shown here at Nottingham Bus Station. Courtesy of David Bean.

Edna Dukes recalled her first introduction to Lowdham Grange when visiting her husband (**Barry**) soon after his first posting as a Prison Officer;

"On a very blustery and rainy day I left Manchester by train for Nottingham with Peter in his canvas buggy ... then a Barton Bus which dropped us off at the bottom of a drive ... Barry had failed to mention that the drive was long and steep uphill with no pavement ... the ground underfoot was thick mud ... I was not amused to say the least ... remember I was a townie."

The Chief's daughter **Margaret Kirk** remembers, in the early 1960s having to cycle from Hunters Hill Farm to Lowdham village to leave her bike at a friend's house before catching the bus to Carlton Le Willows. There was no footpath or lights on the road from Lowdham until the 1990s.

To add to the inconvenience many people recalled the heavy snows and thick fogs of the 1960s. Also we had Foot-and-Mouth, well not us - the animals. When it appeared, we as primary school children had to get off the Clarke's contract school bus at the gates to the New Drive and walk through the disinfectant soaked straw. On one occasion Grange Farm was infected but Hunters Hill farm on the other side of the estate escaped.

The Cocker Beck

The Cocker Beck rises above Lambley taking water from Mapperley Plains down alongside Lambley Lane past Lowdham Church and through Lowdham on its way to the River Trent. The author used to spend hours in the Beck in the 1960s especially as it flowed underneath the two bridges. Under the old bridge leading to Hunters Hill Farm was a small waterfall then a deep pool with an island in the middle: it then broadened, shallowed and boulder filled passed underneath the new bridge of the Main Gate to the New Drive. **Martyn Dukes** and I used to find caddis fly Larvae, a variety of conical freshwater snails and catch freshwater shrimps and bullhead fish from under the rocks with the occasional minnow from the small shoals in the deeper water. And, occasionally, with a bit of luck ten spined sticklebacks but dissapointingly never the more famous three spined. We frequently fell into the sparkling clear water and dried off whilst tramping up the New Drive to get home. Then someone close by upstream opened a pig farm and the Beck clogged up with algae that fed on the pig farm sewage. The Beck between the bridges has now been straightened and scoured and is quite sterile and boring.

Next to the Main Gate before they built that cheap ugly concrete footbridge over the Cocker Beck was a garden that used to be tended by the staff. **Rob Godfrey** from Grove Farm on Lambley Lane recalls this as a source of pocket money in the 1950s after his father showed him how the Lads used to hide their money under the stones of the garden rockery so that they could buy extra fags when they went out alone on jobs in the villages ... suitable justice perhaps! He also recalled the local postman **Mr Cox,** who used to live at the top of Red Lane in Lowdham and always gave the children on his round a packet of Rolos on their birthday.

Ship Shape

In the 1960s the Governor, Commander Noall RN, brought his tried and tested military approach to Lowdham Grange: many of the officers were also ex-Navy. He believed that postings should last a maximum of five years so on arrival he had an immediate purge transferring out officers who had been at The Grange for five years or more. This caused some consternation as did the general rule that promotion meant transfer. Imagine being transferred from rural open borstal Lowdham Grange to an urban high security prison such as Strangeways in Manchester, 'The Scrubs' in London or maybe Dartmoor! Or perhaps a more isolated borstal such as North Sea Camp or Portland. Some from Lowdham Grange uprooted their families and took promotion, others declined. And, a lucky few managed to get promotion and remain. Promotion also meant moving to a better house on the estate. However, some inward transfers felt very differently. Not everyone loved Lowdham Grange or the borstal approach. Some possibly preferred urban living, locked doors and jangling keys with a more officious, formal and unanswered discipline and retribution based officer–prisoner relationship. Some arrived at Lowdham Grange soon to voluntarily transfer back to the more traditional service.

To add to the down side of promotion and time limited postings there was always the threat of being transferred to Dartmoor. There was a list of who was the next to go to Dartmoor. If you were at Dartmoor you could chose the location of your next posting, anywhere in the country. If Lowdham Grange was chosen then whoever was top of the list was exchanged for the Dartmoor Officer. This was an unpopular posting in the days when few officers had a car. Then in the mid 1970s as car ownership increased, Dartmoor became popular due to its location close to Exeter, Torquay and the 'English Riviera.'

The author and others recall that under Governor Noall at Lowdham Grange; the Lads in line, three abreast sweeping the roads, crew-cut grass, square cut hedges, the Lads marching in columns, work groups all around the officers' village; keeping verges and roads neat and clearing snow. The fields were full of work parties and the Lads marched through local villages. The kerb stones outside the Administration building were painted white. The staff, the Lads and the Institution all looked 'sharp.' One officer recalled that:

"In the old days the Governor was the Governor ... his word was final and even Head Office would not question his decision. But in the final years of the borstal it was all uniforms and procedures and referral to region, it lost its distinctiveness and flexibility!"

At Home on the Estate

Edna Dukes gave birth to her son Martyn at home (as was the NHS policy for the second child at that time) at 1 Hill Syke then in 1962 moved to a newly built house at number 22. This had the advantages of an inside toilet, separate bathroom (instead of 'bath in scullery') and hot water from a solid fuel stove in the kitchen ... Luxury! **Tony Bates** recalls that their first house on the Green in 1963 still had the 'bath in scullery' with the fold down work top. When the author left 12 Hill Syke in 1973 our heating was still open fires, a portable paraffin stove at the bottom of the stairs and a small barrel boiler inside the back door for heat and hot water. As **Edna Dukes** recalled "we had severe winters in the 1960s and commonly we had ice on the inside of the metal framed windows".

Facilities?

This section should really be blank as the only facility was the telephone (now just the red box full of books) on the corner where The Green met Hill Syke. I could never remember if and when to push buttons A and B. Shopping was a walk down to catch a bus at Lowdham or from the bottom of the Old Drive - only to have to walk back 'fully Laden.' Even at the end of the 1960s very few people had a car. And some were still without a car when we left in the mid 1970s. But, in the 1960s we did have visits from an old coach fitted out as a general store; I recall that one rite of passage was to ask for something from the back then knick some sweets that were on open display near the door ... no not me ... honest guv! There was also the milkman and 'Barry the Breadman'. At times we also had the Corona Lemonade lorry with bottles of pop pointing out from the sides like some kind of multiple mortar.

As children in the 1960s we (well, me and my mates) enjoyed the fields, the woods and our bikes but as we got older we looked longingly at the privileges of the borstal Lads with all of their recreation and other facilities. Also, upon our school friends who lived within easy access to urban facilities and each other. About half of us teenagers went to school in urban Carlton; the rest went to Southwell, which seemed like a big town to us at the time.

Working at Lowdham Grange

Some of the former Officers have recently recalled:

"When I first saw Lowdham Grange I thought that it looked Dickensian. But of course it was not, either in the building itself or its attitudes."

First view of the Borstal with Rockleys View and parts of Hill Syke, from Main Drive in the 1980s.
Courtesy of Newark and Sherwood Museums Service.

"Firstly there is a great difference between prison and borstal: they should have been different services ... in borstal you had to get to know the Lads and had constant contact with them ... there was a lot of looking after and instilling discipline ... a lot of them needed training in basic skills ... prison was just counting and keys ... they were both difficult jobs in different ways. I would say that borstal work was more demanding ... quite a few people who were transferred to Lowdham Grange from prisons didn't like it and were soon requesting transfers back to a prison, mind you I didn't like my temporary transfers to prisons."

"There were more demanding borstals to work at but working at Lowdham Grange was certainly more demanding to work at than prisons, including Wandsworth. You had to be aware of what you were doing. All of the time!"

"Yes I was given a copy of the Llewellin's 1933 article when I went to Lowdham Grange in 1963."

"The Lads all wore the same uniform; navy blue, almost black, army-style bomber jacket, grey trousers, brown shoes and the blue striped shirt, there was also the characteristic smell of the laundry detergent that they used. In earlier years they wore short trousers so that they could be easily recognised if they absconded."

Civilian Teacher **Mike Barm** recalls that teaching staff were recruited by word of mouth to meet the needs of the boys. He never felt threatened, the Lads were always courteous and welcomed the opportunity to chat as well as engage in the more planned educational experience. He felt that the structured and disciplined family lifestyle gave them systems and self-discipline in the long-term (rather than the short sharp shock of detention centres where he also worked). And, that this helped them to build their self-esteem before engaging with the real world. Teachers had little contact with officers although he recalls that the Lads spoke of them with respect and were keen to give the officers reasons to be proud of them. He thinks that he probably learned as much as he taught.

Mike also paints a lucid picture when he recalls that although he enjoyed working at Lowdham Grange he thought that "recruitment may have been difficult as teaching in an establishment full of criminals who were only allowed two changes of clothing per week, one for work and the other for evenings, spent a lot of time with pigs and were fed on a diet which included huge quantities of cabbage grown on the farm was not high on a teacher's list of ways to spend an enviable evening."

Another teacher at Lowdham Grange in the 1960s was the Headmaster of Cropwell Bishop, then Mansfield Woodhouse Primary Schools, **Sydney Brennan Stokes**. A lifelong socialist and educationalist who thought that "that the only thing 'wrong' with them was the effect of their deprived backgrounds."

"In the monthly House Boards you discussed the Lads who you were responsible for. There were four grades, they had to work for their privileges: when they first arrived the Lads wore a blue tie, they then progressed to red for training grade, yellow for senior training grade and an orangey brown for the discharge grade. It was 'chest out' and a lot of pride when they were promoted and got their new tie. Promotion and eventual release was dependant on the progress of their training, whether they worked well, their background and what was in the future for them, including the views of their Probation Officer who was based in their home town and who took into account the influence of their parents. Very few didn't get promoted. The Boards were chaired by the Assistant Governor. The Governor just signed off the decision of the Board. There was trust then. With Youth Custody it became procedures, procedures, procedures irrespective of personalities or the situation."

"With some of the Lads you didn't know why they were in borstal! Sometimes it was only for knicking a bottle of milk but it was the latest step in the progression of their petty criminality. Many had been in trouble many times before going through approved schools and probation. Many were effectively homeless or had a bad home environment."

"Really it was a big school. We used to spend a lot of time sitting down and talking to the Lads ... it was like a big family ... the officers were father figures ... you really got to know the boys, you would spend a lot of time talking to them, they would trust you and confide in you ... the introduction of uniforms changed all that ... uniforms created a barrier 'Screws and Cons' ... before that it was Lads' names and Mr! The uniforms effectively killed borstals."

"Each House was divided into five dormitories or groups: each had a senior Lad in Charge who was responsible for what happened in the group, you picked out the Best Lad ... there were times when they were more scared of their Senior Lad than they were of the officers ... *(interviewee punching the palm of his left hand)* ... they knew what they were going to get from their Leading Lad if they didn't behave themselves."

"There were still the summer camps, each officer took a camp ... we went to hostels in Derbyshire for a week ... the Lads at Lowdham Grange came from the cities and the countryside was alien to their way of life" ... One officer recalls a nervous Lad waking him on one such camp to ask him to ... lock the external door!

"You were always on duty and worked one Xmas day in two. Living on the estate with Lads working all around you were always on the job and could also be called in at any time. There were no telephones so there could be a knock at the door calling you to work to cover for someone, I often hid when you heard that unexpected knock, and of course when there was an absconder everyone would be knocked up in the middle of the night to be dropped off at strategic points in the local villages and roadways."

"When you were on duty you were always on the go. Some of the Lads couldn't even tie their own shoelaces, many couldn't read or write and had no self-discipline. It was hard work: you even had to go round after morning parade and they had left for work turning off taps and lights and picking up clothes. With adults in prison many were better educated than you and me. But you had to do everything for borstal boys, most were semi-illiterate and didn't even know their 'sums': many didn't go to school but went pinching in Woolworths instead. You were alert and working all the time. It was hard work in that respect too. I have known many people promoted and posted to Lowdham Grange who turned in their promotion to go back to work in Prisons."

"The Governors in the 1960s were very keen on merging it into a big family and involving the families. There were dances and parties in the Gymnasium but these stopped when they replaced the gym floor as it was being damaged by the wives' stiletto heels. There were also Christmas parties and other stuff. Every year we used to buy turkeys from the farm to sell to the staff. **Ted Naldrett** used to arrange this."

"One of the phrases commonly used was 'I never laughed so much since the Governor fell in the fish pond' which referred to when Governor Noall fell off his bike into the water feature outside the Administration Building."

"One of the greatest compliments that I received was from a Lad who said to me that … when I first cum in ere I thought you were a right bastard making me scrub floors and do things I hated doin.' I thought of ways of killing you. But after knowing you for twelve months I wish my dad were like you, I wouldn't have been in ere."

Family Visits

There was a visiting room at Lowdham Grange and the Lads could have one visit per month on a Saturday or Sunday afternoon. And remember, it wasn't an easy trek for the visitors as they usually came by train from far away followed by a bus from Nottingham then they had to face the walk up the Old Drive or a more gentle but further walk from Lowdham railway station via the New Drive. If a Lad didn't have a visitor he did sport.

On one occasion when **Jim Baxter** was in charge of the visiting room, one of the parents insisted on seeing the Governor and would not discuss the unstated issue with anyone else. Fearing the worst and calling Governor **Chilvers** from home, they sat down in his office, where the Lad's mother insisted that she wanted her younger son's name to be put down for Lowdham Grange. "For when he was old enough ... its such a nice place and my Lad likes it so much I thought my youngest would like it." The reported response was an initial stunned and confused silence then "madam, I'm afraid it doesn't work that way." She said "my Lad is so presentable and he is speaking to me properly for the first time: are you sure my youngest can't come here?"

On another occasion a Lad in Malone House came to ask the Senior Officer to come and meet his parents. His mum asked "how is ee goin on" the response was something like "he is a good boy and is getting on well but we have had a few small problems with him and he has been on report this month" ... his head went down ... "you f***ing well do as you are told" said his mother as she got up and gave him such a crack across the face that he was wearing the red welt on his cheek for days.

There was a "big black Lad" who had a bad speech impediment, "a really nice but quiet Lad." One day he hit someone in the showers and broke his jaw - no one would say why. He went 'down the block' and had a month added to his sentence. A few months later the story came out from a Lad being discharged "... I can tell you now Sir because 'I'm on the out' but the Lad who got his jaw broke deserved it as he was mouthing off and insulting you." The officer still retained some guilt about the punishment some forty years later.

Jeff Gittins remembered the excitement of a West Indian Lad on seeing his grandmother arrive on visiting day. However, this soon changed as her opening words were something like "don't you smile at me" as she commenced to chase him around the visiting room brandishing her umbrella ... beating him for disgracing the family. This type of attitude was not uncommon.

In the 1970s there was some reported bemusement from staff about the statistics coming out of the Home Office. Lowdham Grange staff made regular official telephone calls to the Probation Officers of discharged Lads to follow and plot their post Lowdham Grange progress. The resultant local charts showed a significantly better non-re-offending rate than the Home Office official statistics!

On the Lads

There are many similar stories of Lads returning to Lowdham Grange after their release: **Tony Bates** recalls one Lad turning up unexpectedly on his doorstep many years after discharge to introduce his wife and children. Another former Lad came back to Lowdham Grange every year for 40 years after his discharge to say thank you, sometimes bringing his wife and sometimes his son.

There is also a story of a Lad returning in a smart motor car eager to show officers how well he was doing. He had an apprenticeship at a garage and the boss had lent him the car for the day. Needless to say that whilst he was kept talking the local police were called and the car had indeed been stolen. But like some of the other stories it shows some of the Lads needed to be seen as being successful by those who they respected, seeking recognition in return. One Lad rang the office in 'his House' at Lowdham Grange, every day whilst on home leave just to say hello and have a chat. This routine continued for some time after his final release. This and other such stories say as much about the Lads as they do about the Officers and the regime.

Lowdham Grange had continued its role of taking the most vulnerable young men. A Nottingham Evening Post journalist on the fiftieth anniversary of the March from Feltham to Lowdham honestly relayed the initial attitudes of the uninformed. On being told that at weekends many of the boys helped senior citizens in the local villages with gardening: he wrote that;

> 'It was difficult to avoid a brief and suspicious speculation. Teenage hoodlums foisted upon old people, whether they liked it or not. Authoritarian prison officers insisting "Ve haf Vays of tidying your garden' ... "

The journalist continued

> "not at all, was the reassurance ... if the boys don't turn up the old people are on the phone asking where they are. It is even worse if they see a neighbour having help."

Maria Blenkinsop was the Matron of Braybrook House Old People's Home in Burton Joyce where the boys went at weekends and holidays to do whatever work was necessary - clearing up, running errands, gardening etc. She told the same journalist that the residents "trust them completely ... they sometimes say how silly they are to have been sent to Lowdham but it doesn't trouble them to have them here."

Matrons

The Matrons were the 'Mothers of the Houses' a female influence and shoulder to cry on. Matrons also did things like making parcels for Lads who didn't get anything from home at Christmas etc. **Jeannie Berghart** had been an officer in prisons and had looked after the 'Moors Murderer' Moira Hindley, so she used to do officer's duties as well. A matron at Nottingham was murdered, it was a high risk job.

Dorothy Parkinson described her role as being to oversee the general well-being of the Lads and where possible to be a sensible female role model as an aid to their emotional development. A female presence was also recognised as having had a significant moderating effect on Lads' behaviour and language.

And, it was not just the police and male officers who brought back absconding boys. One evening three of the matrons decided to have fish and chips, so whilst one stayed behind to butter some bread the other two set off in their car to the nearest chip shop that was in

Burton Joyce some fifteen minutes' drive away. Nearing Burton Joyce they passed two Lads walking beside the road, thinking that they looked familiar they stopped and called them. One 'legged it' but the other froze; he was told to sit in the back of the car and was driven back to 'The Grange.' On their return from absconding the Lads had to compile a detailed log of where they had been and what they had done on leaving the borstal. The next morning the Duty Officer suggested to the Matron that she needed to read the previous night's log. The Lad had written '... then I was picked up by two old Ladies.' Not surprisingly the 'thirty something' year old matron was not too pleased. And, they didn't get their fish and chips!

A Matron in the 1950s? Courtesy of the Galleries of Justice

A Ghost in the Machine?
Did you hear about a ghost in the tunnel near to the Hospital Block? Some say no such things exist. However one officer recalled.

"At night there was one officer from each House who did night patrol duty and on that night I had to cover Hospital and Penal wing. Occasionally the Governor would do night rounds, and the patrol at the first house would ring ahead and warn the rest of us that the Governor was on his way. This one night I heard footsteps at 4.00am it was pitch black. Thinking it was the Governor I called out 'Governor all is well' but received no reply. The footsteps got louder and louder then stopped, the air felt cold and the hair rose on the back of my neck. I am not usually like that but I shot back into the Special Wing shaking. I later heard that during the war a night orderly had died in the subway. I always wonder if I had fallen asleep and dreamt it. I have never felt like that before or since."

Child's Play at Lowdham Grange
The only facilities in the 1960s and 1970s was the Officers Club – which, apart from, eventually allowing the children of Lowdham Grange staff in on Thursday nights to watch 'Top of the Pops', were out of bounds - as were the tennis courts. We initially had the swings, maypole and see-saw on The Green, which one by one were removed. So we had to make our own fun or mischief in the woods and fields, often

playing 'all day' football matches or racing around on our bikes. The only problem was that no matter what you got up to your father always seemed to know before you got home – someone always snitched on you! You got caned by Mr Chew at Lowdham Primary School for the mischief you got up to at the weekend. And you didn't even live in Lowdham Village!! Also, being pupils at a Church of England School, we were dragged off to St Mary's Church in Lowdham at the slightest excuse. Cold air and hard pews I remember, the lessons I do not.

*At Lowdham Church **John Hague** fifth from left with Mrs Sutch behind. Circa 1970? Mrs Sutch's catch phrase was "Woe betide any child who ..."*

Many of the children had moved to Lowdham Grange when very young, so we didn't know anything else. We had lots of opportunities and places to make dens (sometimes with the help of wire and bits taken from the Borstal scrap yard) mainly in trees or haystacks. And there was an abandoned horse drawn cart in the woods. When we got decent bikes, we could make off down the drives to explore further afield. I don't know who but someone occasionally arranged football and cricket matches with the local villages like this one sometime around 1970(?).

Back Row: Mick Ashton. Peter Dukes. *Unidentified* ? Knight
Middle Row: Jeremy Lodge. Dave 'Noddy' Naldrett. Alan Sewell. *Unidentified* Patsy Knight
Front Row: Martyn Dukes. Robert Wilford, Barry Lincoln. Graham Allcock
Background left: Graham Baxter, under Mick Ashton's arm.

Part 6: A Short Sharp End
1982

The Criminal Justice Bill and Act 1982

Hansard reports that in May 1982 during the Commons debate on the Criminal Justice Bill, Mr Wheeler said that

> "... I think that everyone who knows the criminal justice system will agree that the old borstal system was not effective. It did not meet the conditions of this age or provide the kind of sentence required by the courts."

Baroness Masham of Ilton said during the debate in the Lords on 7th June.

> "My Lords, for about 20 years I have served on the board of visitors of a Borstal, and have also from time to time taken discussion groups in a prison for young prisoners. Most of the Governors, Assistant Governors, Officers and Instructors have been very concerned for the young people under their supervision. Over the years there have been a few difficult patches, and I would stress the importance of well-motivated and fair Governors who can give a lead to inmates and staff. There is no doubt in my mind that, from the inception of Borstal training, some good has been achieved, even though the noble Baronesses, Lady Macleod and Lady Bacon, may not agree with me. One of the best Borstals I have seen is the one built by the boys themselves at Lowdham Grange in Nottinghamshire. There is plenty of space and excellent working facilities ... The useful things which I have found at Borstals are the educational classes; the courses, such as painting and decorating, catering, gardening and so on; sport, and community service. The camping and outward-bound pursuits, where they have

> excellent relationships with staff, are, I think, some of the best. But there is the other side, and that is the problem that Borstals can also be academies of crime.
>
> In all institutions, holidays and weekends often drag because there is not enough to do, especially when there is a shortage of staff. Many inmates have told me that they become far more accomplished criminals during their term of internment - and this is my greatest worry about the new Youth Custody Institutions. The Borstal boys are to be merged with the young prisoners. Some of them may not be very different, but those sent to prison are generally more mature with worse records. Many of the boys I have been dealing with at Borstal are 15-year-old boys. They are still children."

In the Lords on 12th October Baroness Masham also said that

> "It is very difficult to know what to do with a persistent absconder. It may be safer and easier for him if he goes into secure accommodation for a bit. I have had, in my experience of Borstals, young boys say to me, in an open Borstal, "I wish I could go to a closed Borstal," because they find it easier."

Lady Macleod of Borve said, in support of the Bill and without explanation, that she had

> "... never liked the Borstal system and I am gLad that, certainly on paper, it is to be done away with."

Whereas Lady Bacon's points were:

"I have visited many Borstals, Detention Centres and Prisons. I was never very happy about Borstals. Each was trying to do a job of work, but I was never certain that the Governor ever knew quite what that job was. I remember visiting one which was being run on the lines of the rather third-rate public school, and it did not seem to fit in with the environment from which the boys had come ... It is clear from the figures that putting young offenders together in custody does not reform them. The latest [1977] figures show seventy-six per cent of those sent to Detention Centres and eighty-three per cent of those who had been through Borstal were convicted again within two years."

Lord Hooson stated that:

"I come to the first part of the Bill, which superficially is attractive. However, the more that I have looked at it, the more I am convinced that so much of it is entirely cosmetic. Let us take Borstal training. I know that these days it has a bad reputation; it has an 84 per cent failure rate ... When I sit in a judicial capacity I know that our attitude now is that we send youngsters to Borstal as a last resort and not, as in the old days, for training. Borstal is a last resort; it is the last thing that we can try before we send them to prison. It is no wonder that the success rate is now so low, because Borstals do not have a chance to do what they were originally intended to do.

Mention has been made of the Feltham Borstal where, of course, there is a superb Psychiatric Department. Again, I think largely because of the dedicated individuals there. Her name escapes me, but the doctor who is in charge there has been head of the Psychiatric Department for years. To see her handle the Borstal

> inmates is an eye-opener in itself. Borstal establishments have done remarkable work, but many youngsters who are sent to Borstal who need psychiatric treatment rarely get it because very few of them, percentage-wise, end up at the Feltham Borstal, which is particularly equipped to deal with their problems."

The result was presented in less than 10 words in the Criminal Justice Act 1982:

> **"No court shall pass a sentence of Borstal training."**

And that was that: the end of Lowdham Grange and other borstals.

To be Replaced by?

To quote Stephen Jones in the Journal of British Criminology in 1983:

> "The Government's desire to move away from a 'treatment' approach and the corresponding indeterminancy of sentencing is shown in the abolition of Borstal training. In its place section 6 introduces 'Youth Custody."

Lowdham Grange was therefore converted to become a Youth Custody Centre.

Youth Custody: A young offender aged 15 – 20 years, who commits an offence that is punishable with imprisonment for an adult, and which the court considers appropriate to receive a custodial sentence of at least 4 months, shall receive a sentence of Youth Custody. Youth Custody Centres are places where young offenders 'may be detained and given training, instruction and work and prepared for their release.' On release the offender was to be supervised for three months plus any remission gained from the original sentence for a maximum of twelve months.

In the 1982 Act there was a significant absence of the word 'reform': which had been an objective for borstals in the 1952 Act.

*The Administration Building and Tower in the 1980s.
Courtesy of Newark and Sherwood Museums Service.*

The End

Following the closure of the Lowdham Grange Youth Custody Centre in 1991 there was the following exchange in the House of Commons:-

Hansard 1996:

> **Mr. Hinchliffe:** To ask the Secretary of State for the Home Department if he will make a statement on the current and future use of the former borstal establishment and grounds at Lowdham Grange near Nottingham.

Letter from Richard Tilt to Mr. David Hinchliffe, dated 24th April 1996:

> The Home Secretary has asked me to reply to your recent Question about the current and future use of the former Borstal establishment and grounds at Lowdham Grange near Nottingham.
>
> Lowdham Grange has been mothballed since 1989. It is the Prison Service's intention to use the site for a 500 place closed training prison. The new prison will be built, financed and managed using the Private Finance Initiative (PFI). Contract signature is expected in the

Autumn of 1996, with a view to opening the prison in December 1997.

After years of neglect by the Home Office with the bulldozers about to move in a January 1997 a local journalist wrote:

> "Tumbling brickwork, dark empty passageways, broken beams and decaying dormitories .... For five years, one of the world's most historic prisons has been left to the elements – and the vandals."

In place of the historic buildings of Lowdham Grange Borstal now stands a modern high security prison complete with fences, walls and bars.

Postscript: Former Lowdham Lads Internet Chatter

Some of these entries have been lightly edited and anonymised but have been left in the relaxed chat room style.

Posted in 2007

YEH, I was in Lowdham Grange, Patterson House, Daddy Phones was one of the screws, I got sent to the block first day for crying they thought i was going to do a runner i was the only Geordie in there, my name in there was bommer Brown, some fond memories

---

Well it took me a few false-starts, but I think I finally gave all that up when I was in my mid-20s.
I did a turn at Whatton DC (6 weeks, 3 days of a 3 month sentence) then 9 months of a 6-12 at Lowdham Grange. They changed the regime from Borstal to Youth Custody Centre (complete bollocks ... it just meant the screws went from civilian-clothing to uniforms and the sentences were changed to 12 months, with release-eligibility at 8 months and later they introduced parole for people with sentences of 12 months). I then went back a couple of years later to Lowdham for 9 more months, did some remand-time

almost instantly after release, did some more time as an adult the following year (5½ months out of 6), then did some more remand-time. Grand-total of around 30 months.

After about 25, I finally straightened myself out a bit and by 31 when my record was finally clean, I got the hell out of the country.

I'm self-employed as a vendor at festivals and work an average of around 100 hours a week during show-season, 80-odd of it on my feet. I'm 42, divorced, live in Northern California, and have too much going on to have time to think about crime.

I don't think Borstal or prison deterred me in any way ... it taught me to sew mailbags and shovel shit, and while I met some absolute scumbags in there, I also met some pretty nice guys in there who were mainly there cos they were unlucky or did something stupid. Most of them weren't hard-core bad-Lads.

I was one of the youngest in the place when I went there at 17, and now it's 25 years on since I was one of the last Borstal Boys, I still think about the guys I was with in Stansfeld House within Lowdham grange (The FIRST purpose-built outdoor Borstal in the UK – built by Borstal Boys.)

They tried to teach us a trade or something to help us be useful members of society when they kicked us out with our Discharge Grant and a suitcase full of clothes that even Stevie Wonder wouldn't be seen dead in, and they tried to instil a sense of pride in us with sports and other competitions.

Mainly I remember being scared a lot and looking forward to getting my next letter.

I made it a point every time I was inside not to watch tv (cos it was too depressing) but I read A LOT (usually one book a day, and it's a habit I've still got – along with squaring-off my tee-shirts when I fold and put the bloody things away!! Hahaha)

Anyway, I've probably rambled-on more than I should have, but guys, please .... don't romanticise those days as if it were some fun vacation or summer-camp ... it was organized savagery in the disguise of discipline, peppered with slave-labour and shitty food.

On top of that, it created resentment and basically became a finishing-school for juvenile-delinquents. Most of us went in there knowing how to commit only one or two crimes, but we came out almost fluent in burglary, TDA [Taking and Driving Away], *fraud, or deception.*

Personally, I graduated from petty-theft all the way up to bouncing cheques and using bent credit-cards, then committing fraud across half of Europe before I called it quits and went straight.

I was lucky (or smart) enough to clean my act up before I became institutionalized ... not all my pals from those days got that chance.

I didn't get religion or anything like that, although I DID stop drinking about 20 years or so ago.

Oh yeah, one last thing ... I ate my last breakfast ... every bit of it, porridge and all.

2010

Cardboard table and a imagination and loads of time I was in lowdham grange and everthorpe borstals down the block in the two of em they teach me nothing and it was 25 years ago looking back neither of them caused me undo anxiety but I think I would have struggled in a proper block due to my mouth the books saved me not a big selection never the less I found my self climbing everest while residing in hm borstal everthorpe rigby 80/81/82 lost it all do yer bird I was in there in early to mid 60s, did the block a few times, block screws were harry a**** and mr sinton, harry was a right bastard. saw him last in risley

2011

Two of my older brothers went to Borstal in the 1970's and rightly so, they were tearaways and went nicking cars. Did they learn their lesson after 6 months in Lowdham Grange? Well they have never been in trouble since

---

looking for people who were in patterson house in 77. I was there about that time and the ted i remember was in to elvis..? to be honest i went there twice and second time i was of over fields,?.me and 5 others what days...ha.ha

---

Hiya I was in Stansfeld House in Mar – Dec 78, had some laughs, did a bit of cleaning the long corridor when I was in the block for a few days, any of you guys remember Jeff M**** or Krack, We worked on Skilled Labourers, I remember starting off in the woodshop. Played football, PE Instructor when I was there was called Clarke, decent bloke,

---

i was in patterson house in 76/77 remember mr bates /mr spinks /and house matron/ worked kitchen /wood shop then made number 1 i was in malone house in 1976....i worked on hunters hill farm, doing building maintenance...then doing bicycle repairs..also played rugby for lowdham..green an whites...is there any body else from that year still...alive and kicking....?

Hey man I was there in november 1980 I came bout of induction on wednesday & friday morning heard that john lennon had been shot dead, fond memories, at 15 I learnt a lot. anyone in lowdham in 78/79? warner house. i was in lowdham in may 1980 not for long mind as it was an open borstal and i was a bit of a runner, after being allocated in strangeways we all hopped on the coach well more like some old wreck i think it was the same one they used to take you to church in on a sunday, when we arrived i can still remember some Lads standing around singing we wish you a merry Christmas the first thing i saw was the clock the second thing I learned was swamp and if you have been there you will know what it means i cant remember what house i was in but it was 25 years ago and i was not there long,when i did run off it was a half hearted affair me and a mate legged it across the fields the guy who was with me was a half caste from wilmslow any way two screws caught us in the trees not far from the main road after being down the block for a day or so i got weighed off with what ever and told if i tried it again i would go back for reallocation which meant f***all to me,i did try again after having a lie down in the block.any way times have changed my life has changed but the same character lives inside me but

I dont need him anymore but i can still switch it on good luck do yer bird

SWAMP is an acronym for the names and order of the main buildings **S**tansfeld, **W**arner, **A**dmin, **M**alone, **P**aterson.

2012

*hi guys i was in warner house 773 **** (sir) did quite a while in the wood shop under mr whitworth nice bloke lost over 7 months then was offered the job of no1 house cleaner did that for 6 months before my release i remember a mr fretwell he was as thin as a rake but was a good powerlifter also mr chadwick and mr chapman i hear he is ill with a bad heart ?
not been in trouble for over 30 years well never been court lol*

2014

Cannot remember the screws names but f*** what a shi** hole that place was, remember the 'tunnel' one end the gym the other end doctors and the block!!! oh yeah i was in warner 1980/81 i remember **** fat old c**** used to sell us the burn in the canteen! lol can you remember the 11 man breakout at that time? was big in the news? haha.. i was from leicester.. there were *a few of us from there.. 'sparrow' 'Tim' me and loads of scousers.. ohhhh them were the days!*

2015

I came across your site by accident and it took me back to a time in my life that was funny sad hopeless scary and fuckin funny

It seems unreal 33 years later when I think about it but it was real, one memory always makes me laugh. Reporting sick for anything was always treated with aspirin. Repeat offenders had two aspirins sellotaped to their forehead.

Another funny moment was getting off the coach that had brought us from Strangeways at Lowdham grange, a bunch of seasoned boys singing we wish you a merry Christmas and it was April 1980.

Anyway I'm good best of luck if your on the same path.

My girls father asked me what I needed to get out of the shitty world I was in, I told him a job so he gave me a shovel and a brush and pointed to the yard. Up to you ain't it.

2016

i was at Lowdham Grange Borstal from late 1970 to 1972. I was in stansfed house
i remember going on parade then we march to the fields in winter to pick up stones all day
then in summer Digging ditches all for 25 to 30 points a week.
sunday we march down to the church in lowdham. Got in to a Fisticuff got 10 days in the punishes Block 3 days in solitary confinement on bread and water then 7 days scrubbing the tunnel floor. happy days.

2008

I was an Officer at Pollington in 1974 before I went to Lowdham Grange Borstal. Many happy memories and I've met Lads since who have turned out fine.

Epilogue

It is now many years since Lowdham Grange Borstal was erased from the Nottinghamshire countryside. Lingering memories reveal the importance of 'The Grange' on so many lives. Many people who worked there and were posted elsewhere returned to this area on retirement - some posthumously to local churchyards. Others never left, many refusing promotion in order to remain.

The present narrative is an incomplete description of this borstal and the context within which it was born, worked, survived and finally succumbed to political, reformatory and financial pressures. I have drawn together information and contributions from many sources and individuals; personal conversations and memorabilia, press cuttings, academic books, and journals, the Nottinghamshire, Newark and Sherwood and the Prison Service Archives . There are a few items at the National Archives and hopefully more in private lofts, photograph albums and bookcases.

There is no 'Pandora's Box' of information on Lowdham Grange. Later in his life W.W. Llewellin, inadvertently sent his diaries to a local bookseller: he realised in time and bought them back - but they are missing again. The Borstal Governor's Journals, complete from 1930 and at Lowdham Grange during the year of its closure and ready to start their journey to the Prison Service Training College at Newbold Revel - are now also missing. And, in the same way that the building has been 'wiped off the face of the Nottinghamshire countryside' the Ministry of Justice has revealed that

> "...following a search of our archived records in the Ministry of Justice's Branston Registry, we have no record of holding any of the information you require about Lowdham Grange, prior to when it was a prison. Some files did exist, but these have since been destroyed in accordance with Prison Service guidance about the retention or destruction of Prison Estate Management files."

So this leaves just the personal memories and memorabilia of the Lowdham Grange diaspora. I hope to be able to collect and write more. So please send me your reminiscences and copies of old photographs, old documents etc. If you live nearby, perhaps I could visit and maybe record our conversation? If you send me anything please attach a note to give your permission to publish extracts or images – or to say that it is for use as background information only. All that I collect will be returned or deposited in the relevant public archives; whichever you wish. I hope that you appreciate what I have found and written so far.

Appendices

APPENDIX I

William Bernard 'Barney' Malone

December 1908 – December 1943

The picture of 'Barney' Malone in the uniform of the Scots Guards, taken between 1941 and 1943, that hung in Malone House at Lowdham Grange Borstal.

Born in New Plymouth, New Zealand, Barney Malone came to England when he was six, with his mother, brother and two sisters. The London Gazette reports William Bernard Malone gaining the rank of Assistant Housemaster in the Prison Service in 1933, Governor Class IV on 1 September 1938 and promotion to 2nd Lieutenant in the Scots Guards on 26 January 1941.

W.W. Llewellin's obituary for Barney Malone was published in The Times on January 6th 1944 and read:

> 'Captain William Bernard (Barney) Malone, Scots Guards, was marked out for death or glory. His ardent admiration for his father Lieutenant-Colonel W G Malone, killed in action whilst in command of a New Zealand Battalion in Gallipoli during the last war, was well known to all his friends. He read and reread his father's war diaries; it was inevitable that he should take up the challenge thrown out by the declaration of war in 1939. His aggressive persistence obtained his release for war service, first amongst Borstal Housemasters.
>
> He joined the Borstal Service in 1930 and found his feet at Lowdham Grange, the first Borstal without walls; his choice as second in command of North Sea Camp, near Boston gave him his chance to use his great gifts of intellect, of leadership and of driving force. Most of the ideas tried out in that experiment were Barney's. His was the full and varied educational programme which gave many a Lad his first insights into the meaning of citizenship. His was the founding of the troop of Sea Rovers, whose exciting boat trips across the Wash gave an unexpected outlet for adventure for Borstal Lads. His

was much else. The Housemaster at North Sea Camp lived no easy life, for he worked, played and had meals with the Lads, and fully shared their lives. This involved real leadership; Barney never faltered; he inspired his colleagues and the Lads with his own shining faith and devotion.

Borstal progress owes much to him and would have owed more had he returned after the war renewed with vigour and enthusiasm, his somewhat over critical mind mellowed by experience. Those who served with him have the memory of a loyal colleague and a friend of noble ideals and the energy to translate his ideals into action, but Barney's living memorial is in the lives of those Lads – and those not a few – whom he led along the road of life from carelessness and crime to usefulness and happiness. They will remember him.'

Bernard Malone was one of the guards of the Nazi Deputy Fuhrer Rudolph Hess in 1941. His diaries have not been published but are quoted in David Irving's book 'Hess - the missing years 1941-5' (1987) extracts of which were serialised in The Observer in September 1987. Irving records Second Lieutenant William 'Barnes' Malone as a burly, dark-haired former Borstal Housemaster ... one of the Scots Guards' best young officers ... who illicitly kept a personal diary ... Hess initially thought that Malone was there to spy on him. But he came to know and trust him.

He is also thought by his family to have been dropped behind enemy lines in Norway as a spy.

The Prison Service Roll of Honour for those who lost their lives in the 1939 - 45 war, includes:

"W.B. Malone. Governor. Feltham.
Major, Scots Guards. Killed in Action.
7th December 1943"

APPENDIX II

Not just Llewellin

We must not forget the many unnamed staff in the early decades of the borstal system who were recruited from major universities including Oxford and Cambridge: and, those with a less prestigious formal education who supported them or followed in their footsteps. They were recalled by Mr Blom-Cooper QC in a 1987 lecture at Cambridge University when he said that a new spirit in the prison system was most marked in the borstals, under the inspiring leadership of Alexander Paterson. Discipline was based less on any particular system or on punishment, more on education and personal influence.

In addition to Lowdham Grange's Llewellin, many Borstal Governors were strong characters. At Huntercombe Sir Almeric Rich, who was apparently a mentor of the future Lowdham Grange Governor Chilvers; would punish boys by making them pick up flints from the field - and he did it himself alongside them to show that he shared responsibility for their misbehaviour. If he put a boy in a punishment cell overnight he would stay in the next cell to give moral support if needed. Another borstal Governor, John Vidler, did not exactly punish a boy for not working: he said that work was a privilege and the boy wouldn't be allowed to work until he changed his attitude. After three days in a cell with as many books as he wanted, the boy decided he'd rather work.

The Institutions were supposed to be based on public schools; their "housemasters" were expected to be bachelors and worked until 9.00pm with a day off a week and one weekend a month. As preparation for their work they were likely to be sent by Paterson to work in the East End of London to learn at first hand, as he had done about the conditions from which many Borstal boys came. This was the Oxford Mission which provided health, personal, social and religious activities in Bermondsey, which was then one of the poorest and most deprived areas of London.

At the turn of the century, John Stansfeld (the creator, manager and mentor of the Mission) bought land at Horndon above Tilbury to provide a 'rural paradise' camping ground for the young boys of Bermondsey and as a convalescent home for his Bermondsey patients. Baden-Powell visited a Stansfeld camp before setting up the Boy Scouts movement, and was an early visitor to Lowdham Grange.

The annual report by the Governor of Wakefield in 1948 noted that the Borstal Assistant Governor gives his whole time to the group and is responsible for the personal training of the boys. He wrote:

> '"I am more than ever convinced that what success we have had, is, in the main, attributable to the fact that the Housemaster, Principal Officer and the Discipline Staff, are in close contact with the boys, study their individual characters, gain their respect and often their affection and so are able to influence them in a way which would be impossible under more rigid conditions.'

The Times Newspaper in 1923 said of the early Borstals:

> 'Those warders who could only bark were replaced by those who could and would talk to their charges; fatherly men, some of them with perhaps unruly Lads of their own. Others, young and smart, with ideas of drill and gymnastics which terrified slackness and built muscle and fibre on ill-developed frames.'

Herbert Hewitt Holmes (who is credited with some of the photographs in this book) was a WW1 Naval Officer who joined the Prison Service in 1920 and was later to become Governor of Portland Borstal. On leaving Rochester in 1930 to join the march from Feltham to Lowdham Grange, he was described in the Borstal's quarterly magazine 'Phoenix';

> '... his work and example as a House Officer, his

unfailing cheeriness, his ever ready good advice to help along the boy who was down, and to cheer on the boy who was doing well ... all will agree with me that no man has worked harder during the past 9 years for the good of the boys, and to make the institution a better place for them ... his work cannot be too highly praised ... his unfailing cheerfulness and ability to get the best out of the boys ...

His value as a teacher at evening classes was again high ... his seamanship class was I think one of the most valuable and one of the most popular of the evening classes. I have seen letters from boys that have passed onto the sea thanking him for the help his class has been to them and that is the greatest reward any man can have, the knowledge that he has helped another along the road of life ... there was no 8 hour day for Mr. Homes ... he considered 24 hours a day short enough to spend in the service of those he represented.

 I have heard him called a fool for doing so much but I say thank God for such fools the world would be a better place if there were more of them ... Our loss is the gain of the new Institution. *[Lowdham Grange]* it wanted the best and it took our very best first ...'

H. H Holmes at Lowdham Grange with his wife and daughter, August 1931. Courtesy of his Granddaughter

In the 1930s Alexander Paterson said that:

"At the heart of the system is the recognition of the individuality of each Lad. They are not the raw recruits of a conscript army, to be arranged neatly in rows according to their physical stature, to be swung rhythmically in a mass across the parade ground to the beat of a drum. Each is different and a difficult problem. It is because they must be handled individually with sympathy, firmness and discernment that those who handle them must be rare individuals. The strength or weakness of the borstal system lies in the strength or weakness of the borstal staff"

My discussion with former Lowdham Grange officers suggests that the above still held true some fifty-plus years later, particularly as a distinction between borstal and prison staff.

APPENDIX III

The Prison Journal 1978 58: 3 (Pennsylvania Prison Society, USA).

Charles E. Heilmann

Open Prisons, British Style

Some years ago, late of a summer evening, a man and his wife were driving along a country road in the English Midlands, when they spied a man crouched in the ditch alongside the road. The driver recognized the man, but did not stop the car. Instead, he drove his wife on to their destination, near the village.

Then he returned to the place where the man had been seen, beckoned him to enter the car. He meekly climbed into the officer's car and the two men drove quietly back together - to prison, for the driver was a prison officer, and the man beside the road was an escaped convict.

Why had the prison officer not attempted to capture the inmate as soon as he had observed him? Why had he not sounded an alarm immediately upon reaching the prison, even before he deposited his wife at the couple's quarters? Why had he not done a number of other things which would have been uppermost in the mind of a prison officer on this side of the Atlantic? Was it not a dereliction of duty to neglect doing these things? The British would be less likely to see it so than we, for this low-key approach is typical of the attitudes, and thus of the behaviours, of staff to open prisons in England.

APPENDIX IV

The Ordinary Prisoner, 1911.
By Arthur Paterson

Arthur Paterson writing about the ordinary prisoner observed that;

"Twenty years ago prison life of all kinds was a deadly level of mechanical routine, which benumbed or tortured the new offender, and had no effect whatever, in the main, upon the old hand. A low diet, hard discipline, and dull, unintelligent work, these were the characteristic features of a prisoner's life in those days. He has a very different time of it now. The diet is sufficient and of good quality; at the same time it is not ' tasty' and is not therefore beloved by the majority of criminals.

There are three degrees. The:

"A" diet, 'the first and the worst, is given for the first week breakfast, bread and a pint of gruel; dinner, bread and porridge, or bread and suet pudding, or bread and potatoes; supper, bread and gruel.

After the first week the

"B" diet is given. This includes bread and porridge at breakfast and supper, but adds meat or meaty soup, or bacon and beans to the midday meal. On this the prisoner lives for four months.

Beyond that limit and for the rest of his sentence he has the

"C" diet, which still further increases the allowances of meat and potatoes at dinner, and provides him with cocoa in lieu of porridge at night. Prisoners are weighed periodically, and if they lose flesh or strength receive special diet under medical orders.

The discipline of a prison still is, and must always be, strict. It forms, in these days, almost the only really 'deterrent' feature to those who have ceased to care for the disgrace of committal to gaol. But year by year its sternness grows less.

The necessary shock is given to the first offender, who must at any cost be made to feel that there is hardness in prison life. On the other hand, the danger of hardening him by too much misery and discomfort is avoided by a gradual relaxation of the worst features of confinement as his sentence lengthens and a corresponding increase in the encouragements to him to show that he can be industrious and patient, and overcome his weakness. Thus the worst type of ordinary prisoner, the man sentenced to hard labour, has to wrestle for twenty-eight days with coal-sack making, an occupation painful to the fingers, or oakum-picking, the most uninteresting of occupations, or stone-breaking, or wood-chopping, which is trying in many ways, particularly to the small of the back. This work a prisoner must do either alone in his cell or in a cubicle outside where he can see no one. He hates that. During the first fortnight he has to sleep on bare boards, though allowed covering, and for the first week receives the worst diet allowed in prison.

A prisoner without ' hard labour ' also works during his first month alone, but at ' second-class ' work tailoring, glove-making, mat-making, or any other occupation which keeps him well occupied without causing any particular physical strain.

After the twenty-eight days are past the ordinary prisoner emerges from his solitude and works all day in association with others in a shop at blacksmithing, carpentering, mat-making, brush-making, book-binding, boot-making, or mailbag-making. In some cases, he goes outside and delves in the garden, or is engaged in building operations. In any case, he works at a trade, in which, if he stays in some time, he can become proficient. He is with his fellows all day, to whom he may speak on the work. The shops are mostly large, well-lighted and well aired, and in winter well warmed. In each there is an instructor as well as the warder or warders. The instructor assists and teaches while the warders stand like watchful storks, vigilantly observant of loitering, malingering, or breaking of rules."

APPENDIX V

Borstal Routine:

Diet and the Bell Scale

Diet Ordinary Grade

5:50 am
Milk (1/3 pint either hot or cold) and a Biscuit (1 Captain, hard as supplied to sailors in the Mercantile Marine)

Breakfast - Daily
Bread (8 oz), Porridge and Margarine

Dinner
Sunday
Bread (6 oz), Potatoes, Cold Meat
Monday
Bread, Potatoes, Beans and Bacon
Tuesday
Bread, Potatoes, Soup
Wednesday
Bread, Potatoes, Suet Pudding
Thursday
Bread, Potatoes, Beef

Friday
Bread, Potatoes, Soup
Saturday
Bread, Potatoes, Mutton

Supper - Daily
Bread (8 oz), Cocoa, Margarine or Cheese

Diet Special Grade

Daily
5:50 am
Milk and Biscuit

Breakfast
Bread, Tea, Margarine (Coffee may be occasionally substituted for Tea, or if preferred Porridge instead of Tea)

Dinner
Sunday
Bread, Potatoes, Cold Meat, Pudding
Monday
Bread, Potatoes, Beans and Bacon
Tuesday
Bread, Potatoes, Soup
Wednesday
Bread, Potatoes, Suet Pudding
Thursday
Bread, Potatoes, Beef

Friday
Bread, Potatoes, Soup
Saturday
Bread, Potatoes, Mutton

Supper
Daily
Bread, Cocoa, Margarine or Cheese
Lettuce or other SaLad may be occasionally issued for Supper

The Bells

At Lowdham Grange a brass bell hung in each House outside the office: when this was rung the Lads had to react immediately. There were bells rung at standard times each day such as for Lads to get up, the end of work etc. The bell was also rung for other purposes such as immediate roll call

The Bell Scale

1 Jan – 31 Dec Weekdays
5:30 am
Bell rings. Inmates rise. Clean cells etc
5:50
Officers early division parade in Halls. Night patrols leave
6:10
Gymnastics and Drill commence

7:00
Gym and Drill ceases. Inmates to Breakfast
7:10
Officers early division to breakfast. Sufficient Officers of late division in for patrol duties
7:40
Officers early division return from breakfast. Labour commences
8:20
Bell rings Officers late division parade at gate and join labour parties
11:45
Bell rings. Labour ceases. March to Parade

Noon
12:00
Inmates dine all Officers not serving, supervising or patrol go to dinner
1:00
Patrols march inmates to parade
1:10
Bell rings. Officers return from Dinner. Parade at gate and take charge of labour parties
1:15
Patrols go to dinner
2:25
Bell rings. Patrols return from dinner and join labour parties

1 Jan – 13 Feb; 1 Nov – 31 December
4:30 pm
Bell rings. Labour ceases
4:55
Some Officers late division go to tea, return at 5:25 to serve suppers
5:30
Inmates Supper. Officers, early division, and those who performed breakfast patrol go off duty. Remaining Officers late division go to tea.

16 Feb – 31 October
4:45 pm
Some Officers, late division, go to tea and return at 5:15 to serve suppers
5:30
Bell rings Labour ceases . Inmate's supper. Officer's early division and those who performed breakfast patrol go off duty. Remaining Officers, late division, go to tea

1 Jan – 31 December
6:00 pm
Officers, late division, return. Bell rings. Inmates march to chapel
6:10
Prayers commence
6:30
Prayers cease. Inmates march to cells, recreation, classes and bathing

7:40
Recreation &c cease
7;50
Night patrols parade
8:00
Officers, late division, go off duty
8:30
Lights out

Saturdays all year

5:30 – 8:30 am
Same as weekdays

Noon
12:00
Bell rings
Labour ceases. Officers, early division, leave for the day
12:10
Inmates dine
12:25
Inmates march to cells. Officers, late division, go to dinner leaving patrols
1:00
Choir practice
1:35
Officers late division parade. Patrols go to dinner
1:45
March to Chapel

2:00
Prayers commence
2:15
Prayers cease. General singing practice starts. Special grade march to games
3:00
Patrols return. General singing ceases. Bathing commences
5:10
Bathing ceases. Inmates supper
5;20
Officers except patrols go to tea
6:00
Inmates march to lectures etc
6:20
Patrols return
7:20
Lectures & similar cease. Night patrols return
7:30
Officers go off duty
8:30
Lights out

Sundays all year

7:00 am
Bell rings. Officers except breakfast patrols muster
7:05
Inmates rise
7:30
Inmates breakfast

7:45
Patrols (who have breakfasted) parade and take charge. All other Officers breakfast
8:45
Bell rings. Officers return
10:30
Bell rings for Divine Service

Noon
12:00
Inmates dine
12:30
Inmates march to cells. Officers, except patrols, go to dinner
2:00
Bell rings. Officers return. Patrols go to dinner
3:00
Bell rings for Divine Service
5:00
Inmates supper. Patrols return, lock–up. Officers not on patrol leave for day
8:00
Night patrols come on duty. Day patrols leave
8:15
Lights out

APPENDIX VI

Lowdham Grange: A Private Estate

The Land

Lowdham Grange nestles on a hill top on the edge of the Parish of Lowdham above Epperstone, Woodborough and Lambley in Nottinghamshire. The Borstal consisted of three parts; Lowdham Grange Estate, Ploughman Wood and Farm plus Hunters Hill Farm. A total of some 500 acres of mixed rich arable, pastoral farm and woodland.

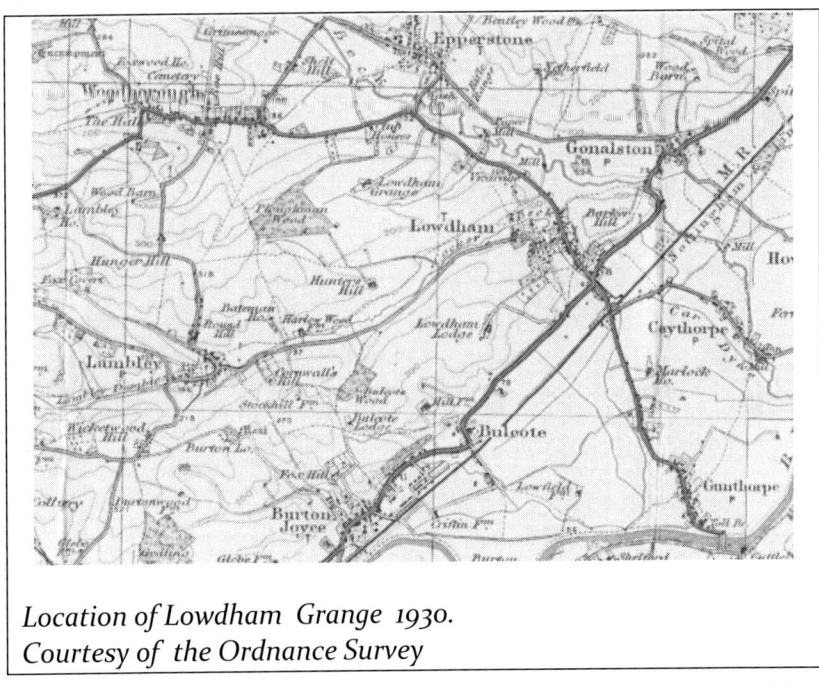

Location of Lowdham Grange 1930.
Courtesy of the Ordnance Survey

Lowdham Grange Borstal Estate was accessed via, what became known as the 'Old Drive' which single tracked rose steep, anonymous and stark from the Old Epperstone Road off the A6097. Passing Grange Farm, the Governors House (now demolished) and extended past the outdoor swimming pool that was built by (and for) the Lads in 1931. The drive ended at the entrance to the Borstal Institution where it met the 1930s built 'New Drive' from Lambley Lane.

The first part of the Old Drive to Grange Farm now provides the only access to the current Prison and creates a sharp contrast to the main entrance and driveway to the borstal. This, the tree-lined 'New Drive', winds gently but persistently from a once imposing purpose-built 1930 bridge and heavy wooden gates over the Cocker Beck. Passing in front of the 1970s built Rockleys View it is joined by Hill Syke and merges with The Green forming a boundary to the Officers Housing Estate. The 'New Drive' - 'Old Drive' junction formed the unmarked entrance to the Borstal Institution. The 'Main Gate' on Lambley Lane is adjacent to the now abandoned bridge and the drive to Hunters Hill Farm and the now demolished, Hunters Hill Cottages. The borstal was hidden from view although parts of the former staff estate remain clearly visible from Lambley Lane.

Other than the main gate the only public view of the borstal was of the tower over the Administrative Block which rose majestically above Ploughman Wood when viewed from the top of Spring Lane as it drops into Lambley Village on its way from Mapperley Top. This landmark was, alas, demolished with the rest of the Borstal in 1997.

Main Gate, 1980s. Photographer unknown.
Courtesy of Newark and Sherwood Museum Service

Grange House

The 1927 sale schedule for the estate described the residence

> "which is approached by a long Carriage Drive *[later known as the Old Drive]*, is brick and slate

built, and occupies a commanding position facing South and South East, with charming, park-like views over the surrounding countryside.

The **interior accommodation** comprises: - On the ground floor – Porch Entrance, Inner Entrance Hall with stone floor, Lounge Dining Room with Bay, 18 ft x 16 ft., drawing Room, 26ft x 18ft., with French Window opening out on to stone-paved veranda with rustic roof, Library, Lavatory with lavatory basin (h & c), W.C. The reception rooms are mostly fitted with up to date Fire Grates.

On the **first floor**, which is approached by a well-lighted Staircase are Six Principal Bed and dressing Room, large bathroom and W.C., with lavatory bowl and h & c water laid on, Luggage Room, two Maids' Bedrooms approached by a separate staircase, Servants' W.C., and an attic Bedroom on Second Floor.

The **domestic offices** include Butler's Pantry with enamelled sink having h & c water laid on, large Kitchen with tiled floor and good range, back Kitchen fitted with range and porcelain sink, Larder with Store Room over, Dairy and good Cellarage, outside Wash House with copper, Coal House, etc

The **Pleasure Grounds** comprise Rose Garden with ornamental Pond and Fountain, Tennis Lawn and Wilderness Garden containing old-world picturesque timber trees. There is also a Kitchen Garden and well stocked orchard"

Although not in the original plan, this eventually became the borstal Governor's residence.

The 1927 Auction schedule notes that, in the north west, the estate is bordered by the Dover Beck at Epperstone which "gives some of the best trout fishing in the County." The estate is also described as being "in splendid partridge country and the woodland is most suitable for pheasant rearing. There is a good supply of both on the Estate", which was also "in grand hunting country", "Ploughman Wood is one of the best coverts in the County."

So as well as a working farm, Lowdham Grange can be imagined as a sporting gentleman's country retreat, with pleasure gardens and country views for the women.

Lowdham Grange 1808 - 1917: Storer

The Sale details for the freehold of the estate for 1919 include the statements

> "the title will commence with the will of Miss Charlotte Lois Storer, formerly of Lowdham Grange, which was proven on 29th October, 1891. The property was specifically devised by Miss Storer's will and it has been held by the family since the year 1808."

Charlotte Storer was born in September 1845, died in Weston-Super-Mare on 24th July 1891 and is buried in Lowdham.

Charlotte's father Charles was born in Thoroton, Nottinghamshire in 1814. He was a physician/surgeon at the General Hospital in Nottingham and Justice of the Peace for South Nottinghamshire. He came from an illustrious County family, whose pedigree has been traced back to Edward 1, King of England. After graduating at Cambridge, he appears to have spent all his life at Lowdham Grange moving there soon after his marriage to divorcee Jane Miles (*née* Stuart). Jane Storer died at the age of 70 at Lowdham Grange on 12 June 1880. Charles remarried in October 1884. His second wife, Elizabeth Clarke, was the second daughter of the late Lieutenant Clark (Royal Marines Light Infantry) who had settled in neighbouring

Epperstone. Charles Storer died on 6 February 1891 at Lowdham Grange leaving his personal estate to his widow.

Having previously commissioned a window in Epperstone Church in memory of her father, Elizabeth commissioned a window in St Mary's Church, Lowdham, in memory of her husband. She moved away from the area in 1891.

Detail of the Storer Window at Lowdham courtesy of the Southwell & Nottingham Church History Project

The sale details for the freehold of the estate for 1919 indicate that The Grange was still owned by the Storer family. There is a pencil written figure of £9,350 on the front cover. The sale was of two hundred and thirty one acres and thirty eight perches with an annual rental value of £325.

The 1901 census shows Matthew Millington, farmer and his wife, lived at Lowdham Grange: also William Shimeed (Grocer) and his family of seven.

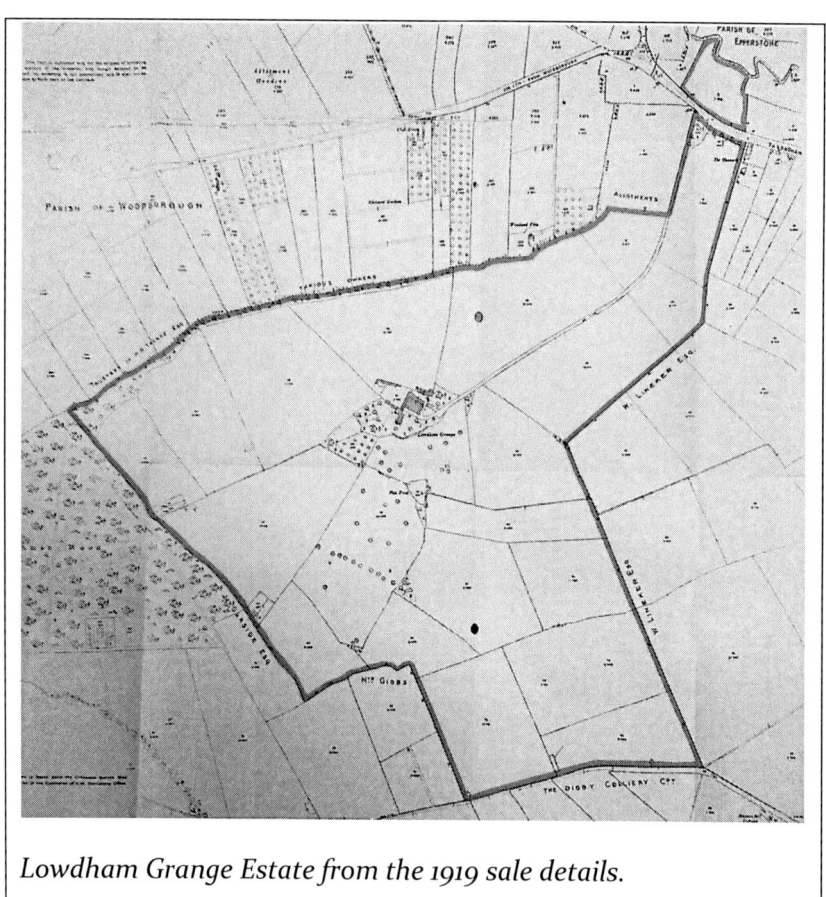

Lowdham Grange Estate from the 1919 sale details.

1911 to 1930: Gibbs

It appears that the Gibbs family purchased Lowdham Grange in 1919. However, the 1911 Census shows a Walter Gibbs (farmer) already living there with his wife, Marian. Walter was born in Hodsock. Marian was born in Elkesley as was their son George in 1900. Walter Gibbs died on 12 December 1916, aged fifty eight years after twenty three years of marriage. The probate record indicates that he left to his wife effects amounting to £1,735 7s. The sale documents of 1919, shows that the land below Ploughman Wood already belonged to a Mrs Gibbs. The extended estate was put up for Auction by Mrs Marian Edith Gibbs and her son George Montague Gibbs with the purchase to be completed on 25th March 1928 when "vacant possession was to be given." A letter from the land agent to their solicitor on 30 August 1927 stated that he knew of two parties considering the purchase and that:

> "With regard to the reserve price I hope that Mrs Gibbs may not be disappointed but she gave considerably more money than the reserve I had fixed, but your purchase of the wood was a great addition."

A reply from the Gibbs' solicitors, suggested "a reserve of £7,000, if anxious to sell."

The schedule for the sale shows an extensive estate of just over 346 acres - 64 acres of woodland, no arable land and "162 acres of some of the richest grassland in the county." With Grange House, there were two, three bedroomed, labourers' cottages at the adjacent Grange Farm and an eight bedroom farmhouse and a cottage at Ploughman Wood Farm.

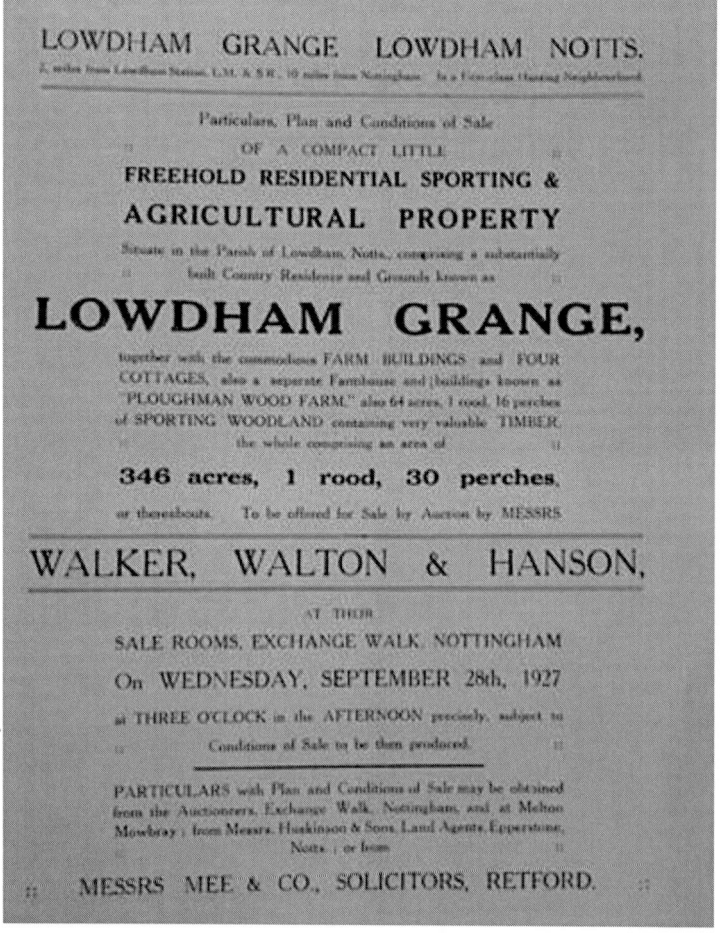

The water supply to the estate was (according to the 1927 auction schedule) "efficient and ample, large sums having recently been spent by the owners in getting connection with the public service", with electric light installed, powered from a petrol engine on the premises. In 1912, Charles Hose Hill, of Woodborough Hall, had guaranteed to find ten subscribers (although only six were needed) to enable the installation of a telephone exchange in Woodborough Post Office. Although many were unsure of the new technology, a manual exchange was installed in 1912 to serve Calverton, Epperstone, Oxton and Woodborough. Telephone number 1 went to Mr Gibbs at Lowdham Grange.

The estate was sold to the Crown for £11,300 and a camp was pitched at the Grange as soon as possession was obtained on 30th April 1930.

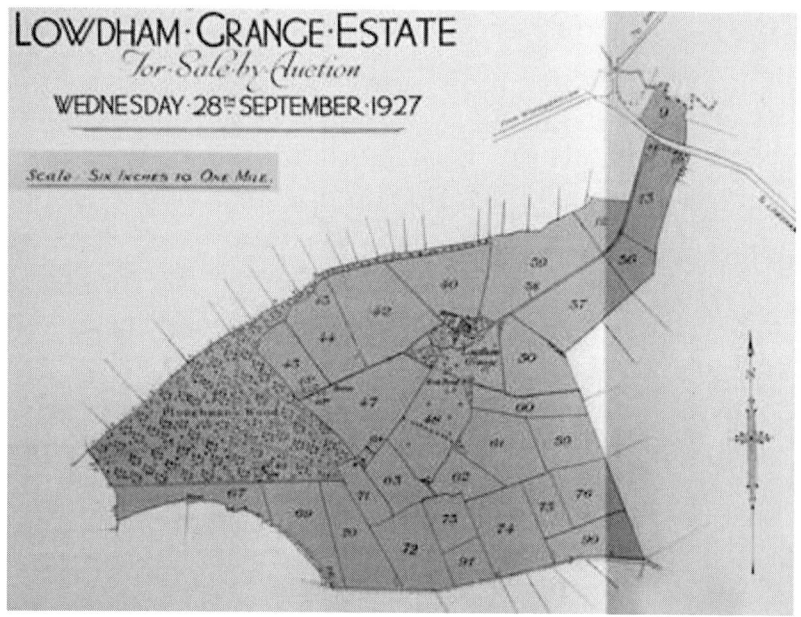

Ploughman Wood

Although currently covering only thirty two acres, Ploughman Wood has for centuries dominated the southern skyline of neighbouring Woodborough village. It was donated to the Nottinghamshire Wildlife Trust by the Home Office at the beginning of November 1996. Records of this wood date back to at least the thirteenth century when it formed part of a much larger area of some one hundred and twenty hectares of woodland called 'Thorneywood Chase', which lay on the southern edge of Sherwood Forest.
Richard Bankes's survey of Sherwood Forest in 1609 for the newly crowned James I shows that today's Ploughman Wood is clearly the relic of Hoverley

Wood. This can be appreciated when tracing the outline of Hoverley Wood on the 1921 Ordnance Survey Map.

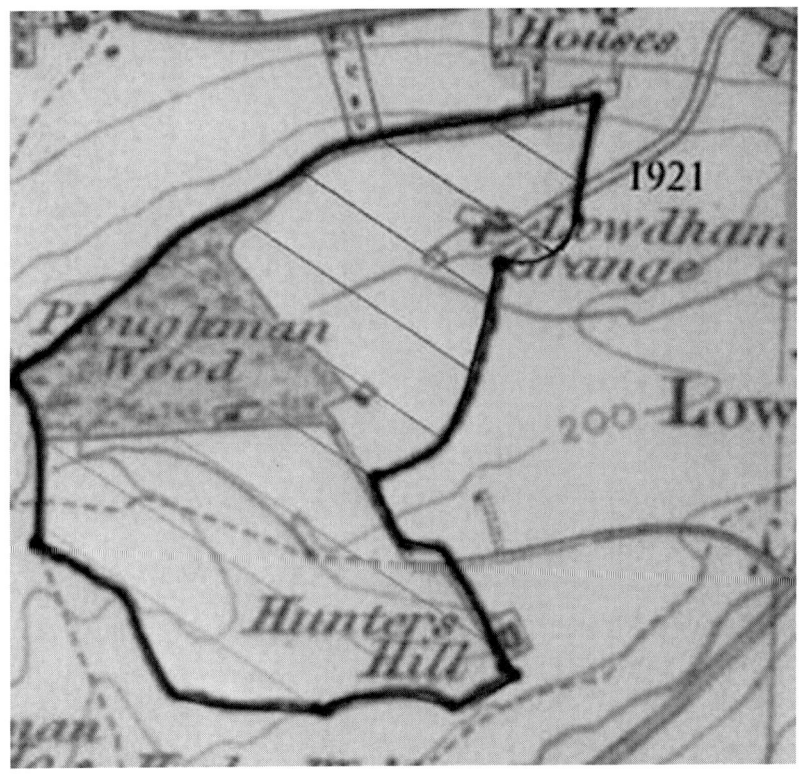

The extent of Howrley/Hoverley Wood, 1400 and 1609 drawn onto the 1921 OS map. A medieval map, records this as Howrley and the fields to the top of this picture between the wood and Woodborough as Hoverley Fielde.

The boundary of the 1609 Hoverley Wood is almost identical to those of Howrley Wood from a medieval map of Sherwood Forest dated circa, 1400, when it was surrounded by fields.

Sanderson's Map of 1835 clearly shows a divided Ploughman Wood with the relic in the area of the current Hunters Hill Farm named Hawley Wood. Lowdham Grange was then known as Lowdham Lodge. The English Place Name Society associate Ploughman Wood through the 1766 Enclosure Award and the Nottinghamshire Subsidies of 1675 with Robert Ploughman and Woodborough as 'stronghold by the wood.' 'Hoverley' and 'Howley/Hawley' are names associated with a wood on the hill or on high ground.

Ploughman Wood is today primarily Oak, Ash, Hazel, Holly, Field Maple and Beech. It also has many plant species typical of ancient woodlands such as Yellow Archangel, Wood Anemone. Honeysuckle and spring Bluebells are prevalent.

The sale schedule of 1927 describes this as most suitable for pheasant rearing and as one of the best coverts (thicket or woodland where game can hide) in the County. It also describes Ploughman Wood Farm as an eight-roomed small farmhouse with two brick built and tiled cottages, wash house with copper, coal house E.C (Excrement Closet?) two-stall stable, loose box, wood and corrugated iron shed for eight cows, four bay implement shed and water laid on by reservoir, 'suitable for tenant to live in if purchaser does not wish to farm the land himself.'

The 1901 census records fifty-six year old George Adcock as the Farmer (employer) at Ploughman Wood Farm. In the adjacent cottage was twenty six year old Arthur Anderson an agricultural labourer. The third Ploughman Wood Farm Cottage was inhabited by Farm Horse Waggoner, Frederick William Beeston all with their families. The Charlton family lived at the farm in the 1920s. There was no indication of the location of these cottages when I lived at Lowdham Grange in the 1960s. But some remember them in the 1950s and a tramp that used to live there in the winter.

Ploughman Wood in 1930.
Photograph H. H. Holmes courtesy of his granddaughter.

Hunters Hill Farm

Hunters Hill Farm was sold by Mr W B Morris to the Crown in 1934. This brought Lowdham Grange's area of farmland to some four hundred and fifty acres. A further four acres was also purchased by the Home Office from the adjoining Grove Farm to give access to Lambley Lane by the future 'Main Drive' and a new, second, bridge over the Cocker Beck.

Decoy

During World War II a mock aerodrome was built between Ploughman Wood and Lambley, which was lit at night to confuse German Bombers trying to find Nottingham. Hunters Hill Farm housed the generator for a further decoy that was on the opposite hillside just over Lambley Lane. **John Watson** remembers cycling as a young teenager along Lambley Lane past the dummy buildings, airplanes and the inflatable vehicles.

Hunters Hill Farm (right hand side, on the penultimate hill in the middle distance) taken in 1930 the far hill is where the decoy above Lambley Lane would have been.
Photograph H. H. Holmes. Courtesy of his granddaughter.

One result of these decoys was that Lambley Village was bombed on at least one occasion.

Hey Chum Got any Gum?

Epperstone by-pass was built in 1933, cutting off what is now Old Epperstone Road and extending to the staggered cross-roads (now a mini-roundabout) linking Shelt Hill, Woodborough with Main Street, Epperstone. In 1932 Mr Knowles bought the land and built his garage near to the bottom of the Old Drive which is still owned and run by the family.

John Knowles recalls that as a young boy during the war the B6097 was the main convoy route from London to Scotland. Being heavily wooded it was easy to hide the convoys from the air. John and his mates used to sit by the road with a blanket and call out "got any gum chum" to the passing troops. "They used to throw us tins, biscuits and stuff and gum! We got nothing from our Lads but the Americans were very generous." When they had a load they would empty the blanket into the ditch behind them and wait for more.

"We used to get loads of stuff which we took around the village especially to the old people."

APPENDIX VII

Planned and Actual Layout of the Institution

The original plan by Surveyor Colonel Rogers shows the later familiar configuration of the four 'Houses' and the Administration Block, but the location of the gym, workshops and the swimming pool was very different from the final layout. Also, it was planned to build the Governors House at the entrance to the Institution near to where the Old and New Drives were to meet. However, Grange House was finally used as the Governor's residence and the Gym was built in line with House 'A', later named Paterson.

Below are two drawings of how the Institution was planned and actually laid out. The first is from the surveyor's original plans and the second is based on a 1939 map courtesy of the Ordnance Survey. Fully annotated versions are given in the main text.

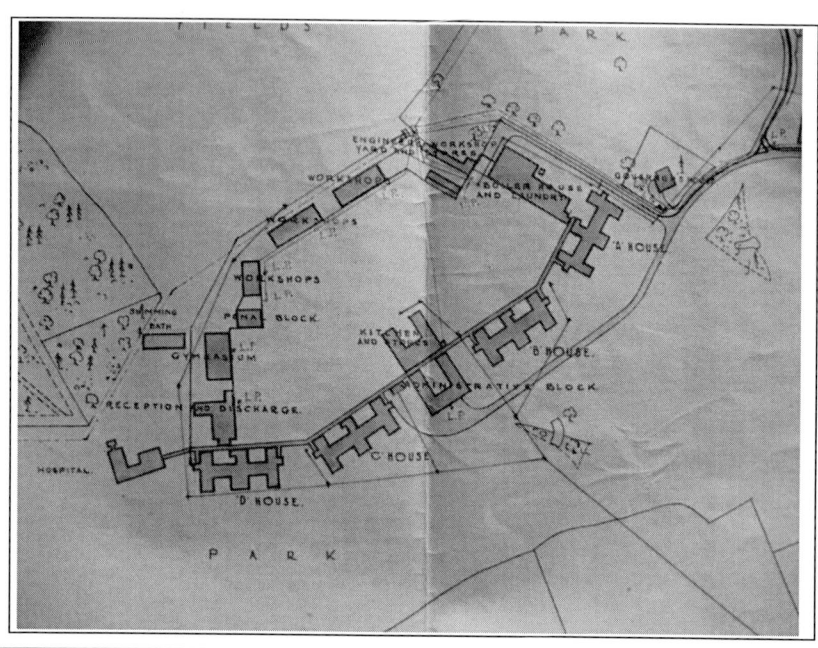
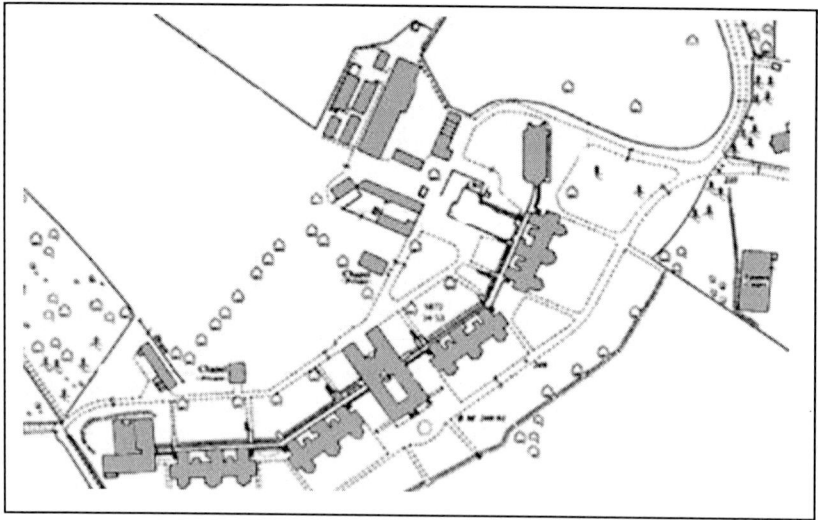

Each **House** would consist of a Dining Room, Games Room, Reading Room, Housemasters Office, Assistant Housemaster's Room, Matron's Room, Blues Room (thought to be a quiet room where the upset, restless or 'blue' Lads could stay in solitude) Leading Lad's Room, Stores, 6 Dormitories for a total of 60 Boys, Changing Rooms, 6 Bedrooms, 6 Bathrooms 7 Sanitary Accommodations. Throughout the papers and plans for Lowdham Grange at this time, class/seniority differences are clearly apparent - here the Housemaster has an 'Office' but the Assistant Housemaster has a 'Room.'

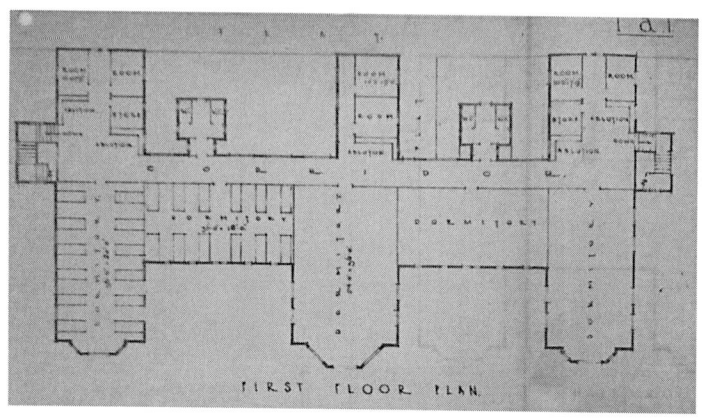

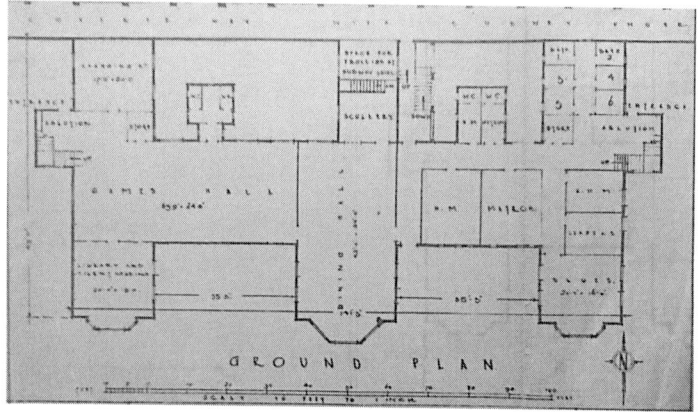

House floor-plans. Courtesy of Jeff Gittens

The rest of the Institution was to consist of:

- The **Reception and Discharge Block** which was to contain 24 Cells, 2 Dining Rooms, 2 Sculleries, 2 Dormitories, Ablution and Sanitary Accommodation.

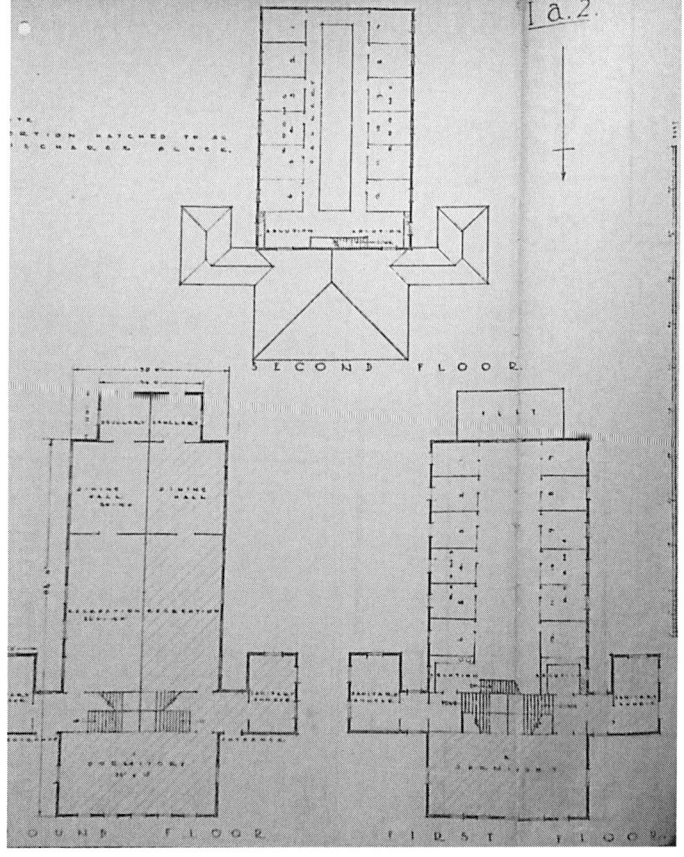

Courtesy of Jeff Gittens

- The **Penal Block** was to contain 12 Cells, an Adjudication Room and Sanitary Accommodation, a Store, Urinal and WC. Also included were twelve Stone Breaking Boxes - in other institutions these were areas where large blocks of stone were broken into pieces small enough to pass through a metal grid. The broken stones were then used for road making

- The **Hospital** was to have 8 Beds, 3 Sick Rooms, Officers' rooms, Medical Officers' room, Dispensary, Surgery, Stores, Isolation Ward for 4 Beds, Nurses Room, 3 Bathrooms and Sanitary Accommodation.

- The **Covered Walkway** with subways and 8 bridges to link the main buildings running in a line from the Hospital and Penal Block, behind the four houses and the Administration building to the Gymnasium.

- **Administrative Block** was to have separate offices for Governor, Steward, Chief Officer and their Clerks; Medical Officer, Chaplain, Boardroom, Library, 7 Class Rooms and Sanitary Accommodation.

- **Kitchen, Bakery and Stores**
- **Boiler and Power House**
- **Laundry**
- **Workshops** for Carpenters, Plumbers and Painters
- Two **Industrial Workshops and Stores:**
- **Plant Room:** Steam Boilers and machinery for the Boiler House, Laundry, Kitchen and Bakery, Engineers Shop and Workshops.
- **Church of England Chapel**
- **Gymnasium.**
- **Swimming Bath**
- **Motor Shelter**

The Tower

It has been suggested that that the clock tower was created as a dominant symbol of authority - to give the impression of an observation tower. It was "the first structure to be built ... the face of the clock being apparent from all compass points ... the vigilant guardian of disciple."

Courtesy of Newark and Sherwood Museums Service

A last gasp alternative?

When the closure of the Borstal was announced in the 1980s the Prison Officers Trade Union put forward two proposals (see diagrams below) for enclosing and securing part or all of the site in order to meet the penal and political demands of the time.

How part of the Institution, as finally built, could have been enclosed and secured in part (above), or, (below) in its entirety. These options were put forward by the Prison Officers Trade Union when the proposed Borstal closure was announced.

Staff Quarters

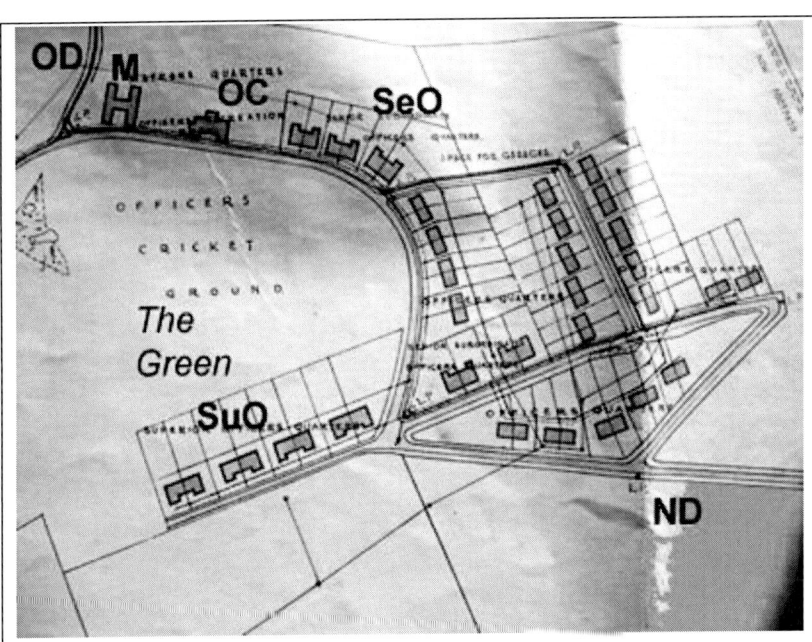

Original plan for staff quarters.

OD - Old Drive
ND - New Drive
M - Matron and Bachelors' Quarters (relocated to Hill Syke)
OC - Officers' Club (relocated)
SeO - Senior Officers' Houses
SuO - Superior Officers' Houses (not built)

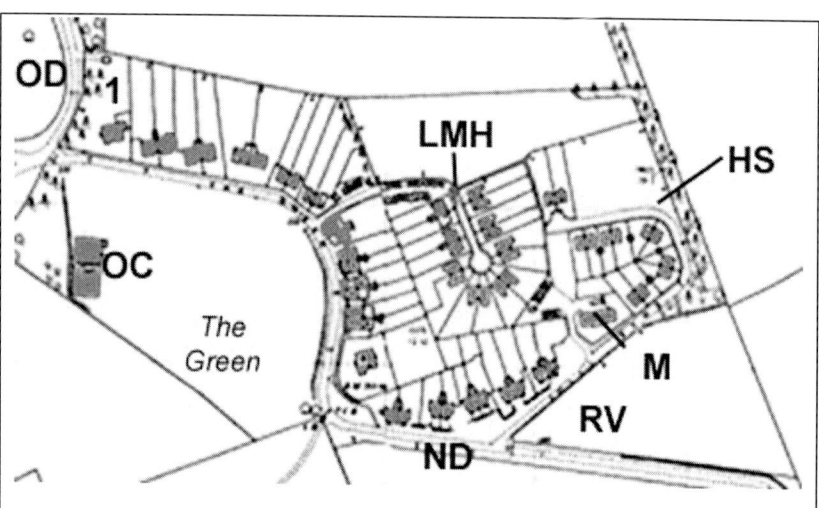

The final layout of the Estate in the early 1960's.
Underlying map courtesy of Ordnance Survey

OD	-	Old Drive
ND	-	New Drive
OC	-	Officers' Club
1	-	Deputy Governor. To the right are the first 5 pairs of quarters to be built
LMH	-	Long Meadow Hill
HS	-	Hill Syke
RV	-	Position of future Rockleys View
M	-	Matron and Bachelors' Quarters

The Officers' Cricket pitch was still in the middle of The Green in the late 1960s.

Building the Officers' Estate. March 1931.
Photograph H. H. Holmes. Courtesy of his granddaughter.

Governor's House: Detached. Drawing Room, Dining Room, Study, Kitchen, Scullery (a room next to the Kitchen for washing clothes and pots, preparing veg etc), five Bedrooms, Bathroom. Note this was to be a new build and eventually became the Assistant Governors house. Grange House was eventually taken over as the Governor's residence.

Also, this was not built in the originally planned location to the right of the 'Old Drive' as it approached the institution. It was built as the first

Officers' House from the Borstal on the Green, which became 'the Deps' *[Deputy Governors']* House.'

This was planned to be the Governors' House - taken in 2014.

Deputy Governor, House Masters, Stewards' House: Semi detached. Four pairs. Drawing Room, Dining Room, Kitchen, Scullery, four Bedrooms, Bathroom.

One of the 4 pairs of Senior Officers' houses - taken in 2014.

Married Subordinate Officers' House: Semi-detached. 5 pairs. Living Room, Parlour, Scullery, 4 Bedrooms, Bathroom.

*Semi-dedtached houses on 'The Green'. 1931. Photograph H. H. Holmes.
Courtesy of his granddaughter.*

Subordinate Officers' House: Semi-detached. 21 pairs. Living Room, Parlour, Scullery, 3 Bedrooms, Bath in Scullery. **Edna Dukes** remembered these from the late 1950s. The bath had a hinged wooden lid which was used as a work surface: this was raised when you wanted to use the bath.

Matron's Block: Dining Room, Kitchen, Scullery, Cook's room, Common Sitting Room, 3 Box Rooms, 2 Visitors Rooms, 6 Bedrooms, 6 Sitting Rooms etc.

Bachelor Officers Quarters: Accommodation for six in adapted Grange House

Officers Recreation Establishment: Concert Room, Reading Room, Billiard Room, Canteen, Bar, Lavatories, Retiring Rooms, Games Room, Store.

The **Total cost** estimate was

	£
Institute	95,967
Staff	55,293
Farm	1,420
Estate Services	3,894
Temporary Costs	4,906
Sub Total	**161,500**

Plus Estate Purchase Price

                      11,300

Total   **172,800**

To these items were to be added other costs, such as the purchase of an additional four acres to allow access to Lambley Lane to enable completion of the Main Drive, legal and other fees.